Gender Loving Care

A Guide to Counseling
Gender-Variant Clients

By the same author

Confessions of a Gender Defender

A NORTON PROFESSIONAL BOOK

Gender Loving Care
A Guide to Counseling
Gender-Variant Clients

Randi Ettner

W.W. Norton & Company
New York • London

Manufacturing by Haddon Craftsmen

Library of Congress Cataloging-in-Publication Data

Ettner, Randi.
Gender loving care : a guide to counseling gender-variant clients /
Randi Ettner.
p.   cm.
"A Norton professional book."
Includes bibliographical references and index.
ISBN 0-393-70304-5
1. Gender indentity disorders–Patients–Counseling of–Case studies.
2. Transsexuals–Counseling of–Case studies.
3. Transsexualism–Case studies.   I. Title.
RC560.G45E88   1999
616.85'83–dc21   98-56029 CIP

W. W. Norton & Company, Inc., 500 Fifth Avenue,
New York, N.Y. 10110
http://www.wwnorton.com

W. W. Norton & Company Ltd., 10 Coptic Street, London WC1A 1PU

2 3 4 5 6 7 8 9 0

Contents

is rather high, and that my expectations for learning much new from this book were modest, at best. I was wrong. I was delighted again and again to uncover new information not available to even avid computer data-based researchers. For example, the second and third chapters are a fascinating inside look at the genesis of this specialized field of study, fueled by the author's personal knowledge of important historical figures and her access to previously unpublished letters and communications from the likes of Harry Benjamin, M.D., and Christine Jorgensen, spanning a forty-year period of time. These two chapters are a treasure trove of medical and psychiatric history unknown to most contemporary helping professionals. Dr. Ettner's long, personal, and professional association with Dr. Leah Schaefer, past-president of the Harry Benjamin International Gender Dysphoria Association and a grand dame of gender study in the world, benefited these chapters factually and enriched the entire book philosophically.

The initial chapter provides the historical context in which to consider the clinical challenges of transsexualism. Dr. Ettner reminds us that it is impossible to divorce the clinical from the political, the sociocultural from the medical, when we seek to help people with gender concerns. This is the first book to comprehensively transport readers through fifty years of medical and psychiatric history with respect to transsexualism. It will therefore become an introductory text to the field in my training of medical students and residents in psychiatry. The early chapters help us to answer the critical question, "How did we get here?" in terms of current treatment models and techniques.

Throughout this book the reader is treated to compelling case examples from the author's wealth of clinical experience in this field. These cases serve to enliven key teaching points in a way that will be memorable for readers. Departures from "traditional" approaches to psychological care are highlighted and explained. Brief sections on the somatic therapies are provided as well, including information on hormonal treatments and genital surgery in both male and female transgendered persons. Although clearly not a focus of this book (maybe next time?), Dr. Ettner mentions the treatment difficulties of gender-nonconforming children and leaves the reader with the unfortunately accurate impression that this field-within-a-field is largely undeveloped.

Arguably the most potent sociopolitical point repeatedly hammered home by Dr. Ettner is the observation that "in an age of political correctness, it is still okay to mock the transgendered." This theme resonates like a sentinel bell in the night to wake up those who may knowingly, or unwittingly, participate in this embarrassing, anxiety-provoked sport.

In summary, this book is an uncommon single-author effort unimpeded by the usual problems of multiply-authored works, which are rarely able to stand coherent whole. It is timely, especially with the inclusion of the new *Standards of Care*, and unmatched by any other works in the current literature. Last, it is well-researched, bold in presentation, and a delight to read. I look forward to future works by Dr. Ettner, as she is clearly a major voice for creative, ethical care of this medically and politically disenfranchised population.

George R. Brown, M.D.
Professor of Psychiatry
Associate Chairman of Psychiatry
East Tennessee State University
Chief of Psychiatry and Director of Psychiatric Research
James H. Quillen VA Medical Center
Johnson City, Tennessee

Acknowledgments

I am pleased to take this opportunity to thank the friends, relatives, and colleagues who helped so greatly with this work.

I would like to thank my parents, Fay and Sydney Cahan, for their support—emotional and material—throughout.

My aunt, mentor, and friend, Dr. Leah C. Schaefer, has been my constant source of inspiration. I thank her for her profound influence in my life and her many contributions to this book and to the field. It is she who graciously provided the original documents and correspondence of Dr. Harry Benjamin from the archives she maintains.

I am thankful, as always, to my husband, Frederic, for contributing his medical expertise and for his unwavering love and support. Likewise, I am deeply indebted to my children, Annelise and Joseph Oliver, for their encouragement and good-naturedness.

Special thanks to Rita Mendelsohn for her deep, abiding faith in me, her invaluable contributions to this project, and her seemingly unlimited assistance.

I also thank her for supplying me with invaluable medical references from the files of the late Dr. Robert S. Mendelsohn, whom I greatly admired.

I would also like to thank my friend, Carolyn Brocksmith. I relied heavily on her knowledge of law and language, and I owe her an enormous debt of gratitude.

Thanks go to Vera Chatz, who contributed material for this work and often fed my children!

Dr. T. G. White has made a great contribution to this work. I am grateful for her research and scholarly contributions, as well as the support and commentary she has provided.

To my friend and colleague, Dr. George Brown, I offer my deep appreciation for all your efforts on my behalf.

Thanks to my colleague, Diane Ellaborn, for sharing her expertise and providing support for this project.

To Dr. Richard Docter, I extend my gratitude for so generously sharing his time and his contributions to the field and to this book.

I would also like to acknowledge Laurie Holder, Samantha Thomas, Bernice and Milton Ettner, Merle and Michael Cahan, and Eric and Anna Cahan for their various and appreciated contributions.

Finally, and most importantly, I give my heartfelt thanks to my editor, Susan Munro, whose belief in me as a writer has been a pilot light in my soul.

Introduction

Few topics arouse such controversy as transsexualism: men who want to be women, and women who want to be men. This complex and highly sensationalized area of behavior is becoming more visible—on television, in movies, and in everyday life. Yet, despite a deluge of media coverage, this remains the most misunderstood area of human behavior.

While transsexualism has always been a part of the human experience, it is not a medical illness or a mental disorder, per se. In Western societies, it has been socially unacceptable, and often illegal, to exercise control over one's body with the intent to modify gender expression. Even in an age of self-conscious political correctness, it's perfectly acceptable to mock transsexuals.

Indeed, people who have the misfortune to be "trapped in the wrong body" experience the joint dysphorias of a body morphology that belies the authentic self-system and societal prohibitions against disclosure of the dilemma. This taboo against acknowledging the condition gives rise to significant distress, to diminished capacity to function socially, economically, and sexually, and to a large percentage of suicides among this population.

Until recently, because of the potency of the taboo against disclosure and the consequences of violating inviolable gender boundaries, persons who experienced gender dissonance remained silent. They were virtually unknown to mental health professionals, and the few who dared to reveal their "secret" were dismissed as psychotic, subjected to institutionalization, or worse. Even the bold emergence of Christine Jorgensen and her much-publicized sex change did little to alter the thinking of professionals: Gender conditions were considered to be evidence of severe psychopathology.

The past decade has brought about a tidal wave of change. Persons with gender conditions are requesting psychological services in vast numbers. What has brought about this complete reversal from stealth secrecy to avid consumption of care? The answer is revolutionary technological advancements that have enabled surgeons to perform state-of-the-art genital reassignment surgery, research that points to a biological, not psychiatric, etiology of the condition, and a venue for disseminating these advances, namely the Internet.

Clinicians in practice today face many challenges in providing care for this population. First and foremost, they must educate themselves about a discipline where there is a veritable dearth of information, printed or otherwise. In fact, too often they must rely on the client to supply this "education." Secondly, few professionals have the experience or background to assist persons undergoing the multifaceted trajectories of gender transition: hormonal treatments, legal dilemmas, surgical options, family destabilization, and concomitant work-related issues. To further complicate the matter, ethical treatment of transsexual persons violates certain cherished canons of psychotherapy. Yet, despite the aforementioned challenges, the rewards of working with this population are enormous. *Gender Loving Care: A Guide to Counseling Gender-Variant Clients* will offer the clinician essential information to meet the needs of this underserved population and move people from pain and isolation toward triumphant living.

Gender Loving Care

A Guide to Counseling Gender-Variant Clients

–1–
Historical and Cultural Perspectives

For there are some eunuchs, which were so born from their mother's womb: and there are some eunuchs, which were made eunuchs of men: and there be eunuchs, which have made themselves eunuchs for the kingdom of heaven's sake. He that is able to receive it, let him receive it. — Matthew 19:12

The most fundamental characteristic of life is gender. When a baby is born, the pronouncement of the newborn's gender, "It's a boy!" or "It's a girl!", trumpets its arrival.

The division into male or female influences many aspects of form, chemical makeup, and behavior of most polycellular organisms. In animals, the gonads determine sex hormones. In mammals, genetic triggers determine how undifferentiated embryonic sexual tissue will differentiate. In the absence of androgenic concentrates, the embryo will feminize. If the androgens are present and circulating, the testicles of genetic males develop.

This organizational model outlines how genes from the parents influence sex steroid hormones that script biological sex. It is often referred to as the "default" theory, because the female of a species develops by default, when these androgenic substances are lacking (Crews, 1994).

Genitals, which are visible in most vertebrates, seem as inviolate, fixed, and unalterable as eye color. Is it any wonder, then, that we are surprised, shocked, or horrified that a human being would tamper with something so seemingly immutable and "preordained"?

Yet, in the past four decades, biologists who explore the evolutionary roots of sexual differentiation have shed new light on the process. They have concluded that genes are one, but not the only, factor contributing to adult animal sexuality. It seems that the hormonal environment during fetal development is another factor that has a profound effect on mammalian sexual differentiation and behavior.

Species that produce large litters lend support for this supposition. When fetuses lie adjacent to one another inside the uterus, steroid hormones produced by one fetus appear to influence the neural and secondary sex structures in the adjacent fetus. A female mouse lying in utero between two males has a higher concentration of testosterone, lower concentrations of estrogen, and a marked masculine anatomy, in comparison to females with dissimilar uterine placement. In adulthood, these females are less sexually arousing to males and behave aggressively towards other females (Crews, 1994).

Researchers have proposed that steroid hormones secreted in embryos organize the brain and affect sexuality. Specifically, they act on neurons, and then link in circuits to provide the impetus for behavioral differences between males and females. In mammals, this link between hormones, brain structure, and sexual behavior has been identified. Yahr and colleagues at the University of California identified a nucleus in the gerbil brain that helps control copulatory behavior in male gerbils. Injecting female gerbils with androgen early in life caused them to develop this "male" nucleus and behave similarly to the males of the species (Crews, 1994).

The organizational concept, which you recall maintains that sex chromosomes have the ultimate control over whether an organism becomes male or female, fails when one looks at other species in the animal kingdom.

Many species, most notably fish and reptiles, lack sex chromosomes. Their gender differentiation is highly dependent on the environment that a given individual experiences. For some, the temperature at which the embryo develops is key. Temperature controls gender formation in crocodiles, many turtles, and lizards. Even though these aforementioned reptiles lack sex chromosomes, their gender, once set, remains fixed throughout their life span. Apparently, temperature acts to modify the distribution of enzymes and hormone receptors in these nascent embryos (Crews, 1994; Wu, 1995).

In species that are not temperature-dependent, the genesis of gender formation is behavior-dependent. In many cases, these animals are hermaphrodites: They embody both female and male gonads. Social environment will determine whether an individual takes a male or female role, reproductively speaking.

Of particular interest among these behavior-dependent species are some sequentially hermaphroditic fish. These creatures change from one sex to another during their lifetime. Since it is known that neural connections between the hypothalamus and the gonads exist in all vertebrates, it seems that these "gender switches" result from signals originating in the brain (Crews, 1994).

Male red-sided garter snakes cluster around females during mating rituals. One researcher examined these mating clusters and found that, in 16% of the clusters, the snake that was being courted was in fact a disguised male, or she-male! These she-male snakes have testes that produce sperm, but also produce the pheromone of the adult female, confusing the more prevalent conventional males (Crews, 1994).

These cross-species comparisons demonstrate that there is a wider range of mechanisms responsible for gender formation than previously believed. Certain seemingly universal truisms are not corroborated by sex-determination studies. Such insights serve to remind clinicians that human gender formation is not an either-or phenomenon, but is instead an obscured, multifaceted process.

From the beginning of time, men and women have displayed cross-gendered behaviors. Recorded accounts date back to Biblical times. Indeed, the Old Testament expostulates against cross-dressing behavior:

> A woman shall not put on man's apparel, nor shall a man wear woman's clothing; for whoever does these things is abhorrent to the Lord your God. (Deuteronomy 22:5)

In 1429, a seventeen-year-old natal female, dressed in men's clothing, employed brilliant military strategies to rout the English from France. Hailed as a saint by the peasants, she was burned alive at the stake on May 30, 1431, at the age of nineteen. Joan of Arc was executed by the Grand Inquisitors in part for her cross-gendered expression (Feinberg, 1996):

> . . . you have continually worn man's dress, wearing the short robe . . . with nothing left that could show you to be a woman: and on many occasions you received the Body of our Lord dressed in this fashion, although you have been frequently admonished to leave it off, which you have refused to do, saying that you would rather die than leave it off . . . you blaspheme God in his sacraments . . . and you condemn yourself in being unwilling to wear the customary clothing of your sex. (p. 35)

After she was presumed dead, and her clothing burned to ash, according to one observer, . . . "then the fire was raked back and her naked body shown to all the people and all the secrets that could or should belong to a woman, to take away any doubts from people's minds" (p. 36).

While the condition appears to be as ancient as humankind itself, the reactions to the gender-variant individual have differed, depending solely on the society in which that individual is a member.

Native American cultures, for example, tend to respect the

gender-fluid members of their societies. The Berdache, as they are known among American Indian cultures, are considered sacred people by most tribes and are elevated to a special economic and social status. Among the Plains tribes, the Berdache performed the most sacred religious and ceremonial rites. They were thought to be "twin-spirits" and to possess such wisdom that even the shaman would ask their advice.

In the sixteenth century, when the Spanish came and "conquered" the Americas, they were outraged by the widespread homosexuality and transvestitism they found to be so prevalent among the Native peoples. They systematically destroyed any artwork that depicted these vile practices (Taylor, 1996).

French missionaries who, in the eighteenth century, came to convert the Native Americans, were puzzled by the Native view of the Berdache. They categorically condemned the Berdache for acting like women, and could not comprehend their prominent role in the non-white world (Williams, 1986).

> Through what superstition I know not, some Illinois while yet young, assume female dress, and keep it all their life. There is a mystery about it, for they never marry, and glory in debasing themselves to do all that is done by women; yet they go to war, though not allowed to use a bow and arrow, only a club. They are permitted to sing but not to dance; they attend councils and nothing can be decided without their advice; finally, by profession of an extraordinary life, they pass for manitous, or persons of consequence. (Sutton, 1970)

According to Taylor in *The Prehistory of Sex*, early societies, dating as far back as the Iron Age, used biological means to manipulate gender (1996). Ovid, the first-century B.C. poet, refers in verse to the extract of "stuff from a mare in heat" (Taylor, 1996). (Premarin®, a commonly used drug by transsexuals today, is extracted from the urine of pregnant mares.)

Hippocrates described a group of Scythians, called Enarees,

who may have been created by amputating the sex organs. Throughout ancient Europe, Asia, and Africa, individuals with altered or mutilated genitals appeared. Similar to the Berdache, they include the mahus in Polynesia, the hirjas of modern India, and the castrati of Europe. Dramatic physical modifications are not a recent phenomenon by any means (Dynes, 1990; Taylor, 1996).

The Hawaiian language contains no female or male adjectives or articles, and even proper names are androgynous. This reflects the Polynesian emphasis on integration and balance of the male and female gods. The notion of gendered polarity—of opposite sexes—is foreign to Hawaiian thought. The mahu embody this ancient Polynesian principle of spiritual duality and are viewed as an honored intermediate sex, integral to Hawaiian culture and cosmology (Robertson, 1989):

> Sometimes Mother Nature cannot make up her mind, whether to make a man or a woman, even in Polynesia, so she mixes up a little of the male with some of the female element. (p. 313)

The mahu phenomenon cannot be reduced to any parallel Western concept of gender. Many women in Hawaii were raised as boys by parents or grandparents to keep them free of sexual liaisons with men. In earlier generations, these girls would have performed tasks of healing or the sacred hula dances. Similarly, elderly Hawaiian men who begot many sons but no daughters often decided to raise the youngest boy as a girl. In this way, they were able to provide additional labor for women's tasks. This practice seems to date back to ancient times (Robertson, 1989).

The mahu of Hawaii assume a large role in history and legend. Today's mahu population contains an astounding variety of individuals. The term mahu can refer to women who dress and work as men, men who dress and work as women, women or men who dress to conceal their biological classification, women who only associate with other women, men who dress "festively," men who undergo hormonal or surgical procedures, true hermaphrodites, or those who Westerners call "gay." Parents often choose to put their children in the care of mahu, for mixed gender people are deemed to be particularly compassionate and creative (Robertson, 1989).

The castrati of Europe were male singers who were castrated between the ages of six and eight, to preserve the soprano or contralto range of their young voices. The earliest origins of this practice were recorded in the sixteenth century. Castratis figure prominently in the history of opera, from its very beginning (Sadies, 1980). A ban on the appearance of women on stage caused the castratis to reach a pinnacle of popularity between 1650 and 1750. Interestingly, although the Church prohibited mutilation, the musical needs of the Church prevailed over the sanction against such amputations. Since castratis were most likely selected from among the poor, in exchange for payment to the parents, or were orphans, the practice of operating on these children was clandestine, albeit widespread. During the eighteenth century, some 4,000 operations occurred (Barbier, 1996; Sadies, 1980). The following account indicates the secrecy of these surgeries (Sadies, 1980):

> I inquired throughout Italy at what place boys were chiefly qualified for singing by castration, but could get no certain intelligence. I was told at Milan that it was at Venice; at Venice that it was at Bologna; but at Bologna the fact was denied, and I was referred to Florence; from Florence to Rome, and from Rome I was sent to Naples. The operation is most certainly against law in all these places, as well as against nature; and all the Italians are so much ashamed of it, that in every province they transfer it to some other. (p. 876)

Like Europe, the history of India is replete with references to people of unusual gender characteristics. The *Kama Sutra* devoted a whole chapter to eunuch courtesans. Two kinds of eunuchs were discussed by Vatsayana, author of the *Kama Sutra,*—those who had "a bust" and were "without hair" appearing as women, and others who took a male form and "imitated men's beards" (Vatsyayana, 1961).

In modern India, a group of people known as hirjas are rarely discussed, and little is known about them. Like the mysterious snake-charmers, they are a bit of India's exotica that the populace would like to ignore. Yet some journalists estimate that there are a million of these hirjas, who play a fascinating and complex role in modern India (Jaffrey, 1996).

The word "hirja" is said to translate as "neither man nor woman." Tolerated but scorned, they are thought to bring good luck to newlyweds, and yet hirjas are often accused of being kidnappers. A mystery in India is how they know when, and where, a wedding reception will take place, for they attend, uninvited. At these weddings, they dance but cannot sing, and perform unusual gestures, often jeering at guests. Finally, they are paid to leave (Jaffrey, 1996).

One Indian-born journalist describes the frustration of trying to get information about this taboo subject. She is told by concerned relatives that even inquiring about the hirjas may render her unsuitable as a marriage partner. Persisting nevertheless, she bribes an alleged "unionizer" of the hirjas. But, after paying him two thousand dollars, she is still unclear as to whether his story is true or part of the "national cover-up" (Jaffrey, 1996):

> I suggested that the names . . . implied a connection to Islam.
> 'No,' said Bhola. 'This is strictly Hindu, madam.'
> 'Why, today,' I asked, 'does one become a eunuch?'
> 'Because,' said Bhola, 'they think of themselves as women. They grow up wearing women's clothes. They are trans-

sexuals. . . . There are transsexuals all over the world, and
India is no exception.'
'They want to be castrated?'
'They volunteer to be castrated,' said Bhola.
'At what age?'
'Fifteen, sixteen,' said Bhola.
'Volunteer, or are kidnapped?'
Bhola took great offense at the suggestion. (pp. 30–31)

In contemporary societies, the predominant attitudes
towards gender-variant individuals are ridicule, disdain, and
outright contempt, with few exceptions. The Netherlands are
unique in their acceptance of their gender-variant citizens. They
"mainstream" transsexuals into society and extend public
health benefits to pay for their medical expenses. Another
notable exception to the almost universal rejection of the transsexual is Burma. Men who dress like women play an important
role in the religious life of the Burmese (Coleman, Colgan, &
Gooren, 1992).

In the Western world, however, and particularly in America,
the transsexual is the equivalent of the Biblical leper (Ettner,
1996). Shunned and ostracized, these individuals are the only
group that it is still politically correct to openly mock. In fact,
they are the only group specifically excluded from the
Americans with Disabilities Act. Why?

Cultural historians argue that, as societies became more
patriarchal and stratified into economic classes, gender-specific
clothing became the barometer of an individual's status. Lack
of property and wealth caused certain groups of people to
become enslaved by, or subordinated to, the noble and royal
classes (Feinberg, 1996; Garber, 1993; Taylor, 1996). As indus-
trialization flourished, gender-variant people were no longer
considered spiritual or gifted beings, but rather were condemned for their lack of uniformity. The ancient, inextricable
connection between the gods, spirituality, shamanism, and
transsexuality unraveled.

Perhaps the answer also lies in our society's inability to separate gender from sexuality. If we as a society are homophobic, we are morbidly "transphobic," to say the least. American mores strictly prohibit the crossing of the inviolable gender line.

Despite the assumptions that underlie this venomous American tribal consciousness, in truth, transsexuality, unlike homosexuality, contains no implicit sexuality in its expression. It is, by its very nature, solitary behavior. It does not involve a partner. Moreover, it is harmless behavior. The individual who makes a gender transition poses no real threat to any other person, only the perceived social threats that are attendant in this society.

Aesop, who lived in Greece in the sixth century B.C., used his fables to win negotiations in the courtroom and to teach morality. Interestingly, he uses the concept of gender transition to entreat people to practice empathy and to live by the "golden rule." In the fable "The Hyenas," Aesop alludes to the ancient myth that the hyenas changed gender every year. When a male hyena attempts an "unnatural act" with a female, she reminds him to "remember that what you do to me will soon be done to you" (Temple, 1998). As the foregoing discussion demonstrates, however, there is little application of the "golden rule" with regard to the transgendered.

This historical and pancultural backdrop serves to remind the clinician that individuals who feel betrayed by their bodies have always been a part of the human landscape. Only within this broad framework, released from the distracting and prejudicial social conventions of geographical and temporal context, can one gain the necessary perspective to understand gender dysphoria.

–2–
Transsexualism in the United States

I ask myself, in mercy, or in common sense, if we
cannot alter the conviction to fit the body, should we
not, in certain circumstances, alter the body to fit the
conviction? — Harry Benjamin to Jan Morris

In 1910, the German sexologist Magnus Hirschfield published *Die Transvestiten*. This classic monograph described the cross-gender behavior that had been noted in German medical literature as early as 1877 and referred to as "metamorphosis sexualis paranoia" by Kraft-Ebbing. When the book was translated into English, the term "transvestite" originated. It was used liberally to describe any form of gender-variant behavior (Pauly, 1992).

Havelock Ellis, who studied sexual perversions, coined the phrases "inversion" and "eonism" to describe the condition (1936a). In early twentieth-century America, cases of eonism were not publicized, and neither the public nor the medical profession encountered these individuals or was even remotely aware of their existence. However, *Sexology* magazine occasionally would receive letters to the editor from desperately unhappy individuals asking if treatment or surgeries existed to alter men who wanted to be women or vice versa. These letters from "sexual inverts" appeared as early as 1930. The inquiries were answered simply: No treatments for conversion exist (Myerowitz, 1998).

● ● ●

In 1911, a young physician and scientist named Harry Benjamin left his native Germany for New York, to conduct research on tuberculosis. Soon after settling, Dr. Benjamin became disenchanted with the poor quality of research that was being carried out in the United States. Disappointed, he left New York and set sail for his homeland. Destiny was to intervene, however. World War I erupted, and Benjamin returned to the safe harbor of New York, where he would live out the remainder of his 101 years.

Harry Benjamin's primary interest was the role of glands in the aging process. Fortuitously, in 1916, Harry Benjamin met Joseph Frankel at Columbia University. The two physicians, who quickly discovered a common interest in the function of glands, met weekly to explore their shared pursuits. According to Benjamin, "Frankel was interested in glands when nothing was known about the pituitary; no one had even heard of the pineal, and little was known about the thyroid" (personal communication). Frankel went so far as to assert that glandular action was the regulator of personality. But for Benjamin, Frankel's real contribution was his discovery that cessation of sexual gland functioning marked the onset of old age (Schaefer & Wheeler, 1987b).

Benjamin passionately pursued his joint interests in endocrinology and gerontology. In 1921, he met Professor Eugen Steinach in Vienna. Through collaboration with Steinach, Benjamin ascertained that "vasoligation" (ligation of the vas deferens) had a restorative effect in elderly men, an observation that presaged the eventual use of hormone replacement therapy in the aged. He credited Steinach with the discovery of the "puberty gland" and the interstitial hormone-producing cells of the testes. Steinach also pioneered experiments in which he "changed the sex" of animals through castration and implantation of the opposite sex glands—a harbinger of a new discipline that would emerge, forged largely by serendipity (Meyerowitz, 1998; Schaefer & Wheeler, 1987b).

These early observations and experiments not only fueled

Benjamin's scientific ardor, but also interwove seemingly disparate areas of medical inquiry: endocrinology, gerontology, and sexology. Benjamin applied this evolving and accumulating knowledge: He urged chemists Cassimir Funk and Benjamin Harrow to isolate an androgenic steroid from human urine, which he used to treat male impotence (Schaefer & Wheeler, 1987b).

Benjamin spent the next decade of his life lecturing and treating aging patients with testosterone and estrogen. In 1943, he introduced the term "gerontotherapy" to describe this application of endocrine therapy to geriatrics (Schaefer & Wheeler, 1987b). But it was an incident that took place several years later that would shift the focus of Benjamin's career, earn him a place in history, and change the lives of countless people.

This defining event occurred in San Francisco, in the summer of 1948. Alfred Kinsey and some of his colleagues were taking sex histories for their ongoing research. By chance, Kinsey and Benjamin, who were colleagues and friends, happened to be staying in the same hotel. Kinsey interviewed a young man who presented a situation that Kinsey had never before encountered: He claimed that he wanted to change his sex! Kinsey somehow felt that Benjamin might be a good choice for a referral, and he asked the endocrinologist to meet with the young man (Schaefer & Wheeler, 1987a).

Van was twenty-three years old and was accompanied by his mother. She pleaded with Benjamin to help the child, entreating, "Look at this boy, he's not a boy! You've got to do something to help my son be a girl!" The story that Van told was bizarre, yet wrenching: Until age two, Van dressed as a boy. At three years of age, with no encouragement, he began to wear girl's clothing. This continued throughout grade school. Special toilet arrangements were made, as psychiatrists reassured the parents that this highly intelligent boy would soon outgrow this phase (Schaefer & Wheeler, 1987a).

The high school refused to accommodate the cross-dressed child, so Van remained home "doing women's work," rather than attend school. He was insistent that he be treated as a girl; when he was not, he would lose all emotional control, often becoming violent.

The records reveal that Van was institutionalized by the courts the year before his meeting with Benjamin and Kinsey. According to those records, Van had a persistent desire to be a girl from childhood on. He never wavered in his dream to change physically, "praying constantly for such a miracle" so he "could marry, have a house, and children." His manner of thinking was undeniably and exclusively female, and he refused to accept the reality that such a change was socially impossible. Van attained no sexual excitement from wearing women's clothing and never had an erection, even nocturnally, or ever masturbated.

Benjamin was unable to find a urologist who would surgically convert Van, and urged him to go to Germany where castration and amputation techniques were being performed. It is remarkable, in view of subsequent developments, that medical consultants in the United States did not oppose a surgical solution for this first patient. However, the Attorney General of Wisconsin interpreted state law to define such surgery as "mayhem," and conversion surgery was therefore prohibited in the United States at that time.

Van made three trips to Europe between the years of 1953 and 1958. Calling herself Susan, she had a series of surgeries that culminated with the construction of a neovagina, lined with skin of the thigh. Susan and her mother moved to Canada and were never heard from again.

A year after meeting Van/Susan, in 1949, Kinsey once again made a referral to Benjamin. This too, proved to be an astonishing situation, as it was a couple who were married to one another, but both living in the opposite gender. A

California clinic tried to locate this couple to determine certain legalities of name and gender status. The clinic wrote to Harry Benjamin:

> . . . both partners became transvestites; the former wife became legally a man and had the marriage annulled. The pair still live together, however, in reversed roles; the former wife takes the role of husband and breadwinner, and the former husband now stays at home and keeps house.

Benjamin provided hormonal therapy for both partners for the remainder of their lives. He also counseled them in psychological matters. Barbara, the male-to-female transsexual, grew increasingly hopeless about the possibility of ever finding a surgeon who would assist her. Benjamin wrote to her imploring her not to lose heart. "You waited this long, wait a few months longer . . . things may change. . . . We have to find a way to help you within the presently existing possibilities." In 1956, at the behest of Benjamin, Dr. Elmer Belt performed peotomy on Barbara, becoming one of the earliest known American physicians to do sex-reassignment surgery.

In 1953, five years after he saw his first transsexual patient, Benjamin gave a lecture on this subject entitled, "Transsexualism and Transvestism as Psycho-Somatic and Somatopsychic Syndromes." At that time, Benjamin had seen ten gender dysphoric patients (Schaefer & Wheeler, 1987a).

By December of 1965, Benjamin had seen three hundred and seven such patients. They would serve as the sample for his book. Finally, with the publication of *The Transsexual Phenomenon* (1966), the silence was broken for the thousands whom ignorance had rendered mute.

In the final fifteen years of his practice, Dr. Benjamin would treat an additional one thousand patients for gender dysphoria. By then, he had established a world-wide network of practitioners to assist with all aspects of the condition, for he well understood the intrinsic intertwining of the psychological and medical aspects of transsexualism.

Harry Benjamin reconstructed a taboo area of human behavior into a medical specialty, but it was his seventh patient who would deconstruct existing notions of gender permanence.

In 1952 a young G. I. left the United States to go to Europe and become a female. Christine Jorgensen described her return:

> I didn't return from Europe until March of 1953 and I encountered a mountain of mail, and I do mean a mountain—thousands and thousands of letters, many of which were from people who had problems that were similar to mine—and it was incredible and in that mountain of mail was a letter from Harry Benjamin whom I had never heard of before and he told me that he was guiding people . . . concerning transsexuality. And it was an absolute godsend for me because I was getting these thousands and thousands of letters and my mother was the one who was answering them. . . . I could recommend Harry to all these thousands of people who contacted me. So the deluge fell onto poor Harry's shoulders. (1988)

Here is the letter Benjamin wrote to Christine Jorgensen:

February 16, 1953

Dear Miss Jorgensen:

These lines are written to you in the interest of some of my patients and naturally also of those whose emotional problems, nobody understands better than you do.

Frankly I am worried over the effect your story and publicity may have in some instances. I had a few rather frantic phone calls and letters recently. Therefore, I would be grateful to you if you would tell me how you are handling the innumerable communications that undoubtedly came to you. Don't they all indicate hopefulness yet utter frustration?

In my many years of practice of sexology and endo-crinology, problems similar to yours have been brought to me frequently. I need not tell you how profoundly disturbed some of these people are. Naturally they identify themselves with you. Can I tell them that you will answer their pleas with a personal note, a friendly non-committal form-letter perhaps, but—for psychological reasons—bearing your signature? That would help enormously. Or have you formulated another plan? Can I be of any assistance? If so please feel free to call on me.

Most sincerely and earnestly yours,

Harry Benjamin, M.D.

While "thousands and thousands" wrote to Christine Jorgensen for support and guidance, countless others did not. Many were simply too young to contact her, but they were indelibly marked by her courageous public disclosure of her transition from male to female.

Joe D. is 50 and has a lifelong history of gender dysphoria. Like many contemporary adults, he will never forget the life-altering day when he finally found a name for his pain: trans-sexualism.

> When I was six years old and in the first grade I remember coming home from school for lunch one day. While home I heard something, I believe it was on the radio, about Christine Jorgensen and that doctors had surgically transformed a man into a woman. On my way back to school that's all I could think about. It made such an impact on me that I can vividly remember the sort of day it was. I remember looking up at the sky and saying, "God, maybe someone can do that for me some day."

On April 14, 1953, Christine Jorgensen became a patient of Harry Benjamin. His notes describe her as a 27-year-old trans-

17

sexual, "operated." What Dr. Benjamin knew, and the media did not, was that Christine Jorgensen's surgical conversion was only partially completed. She was in need of vaginoplasty.

July 17, 1953

Dear Harry,

I received your letter today. It was nice hearing from you. Things are going fine here. I am preparing for my public appearances starting the 10th of August in Pittsburgh. I had a letter from Dr. Thoreak yesterday too.
Quote. . .

"While the transplantation of ovarian tissue may be of endocrinologic value I have consulted with my advisers and I find that the laws of the state of Illinois prohibit performing any operations on the genital apparatus of this nature. This is a decision that I have to abide by."

This is of course a rather easy way of saying I am afraid to try it. But then I can well understand that should the publicity get out he would be subject to the most severe criticism and obviously does not believe enough in what he is doing to take that chance. But then I can't see any reason why he should take that chance. As before, three years ago I made the fatal mistake of going to a practitioner rather than a man of science. There are those who read the books and those who write them. I guess that I will go to Europe for the next operation. You know, Dr. Benjamin, courage is a rare thing. They [the medical profession] are all willing to have their comments quoted provided that there is absolutely no chance of any repercussions but to stand up and fight would affect their rather lucrative practices. You know, I just can't help thinking about the beginning of medicine and the progressive steps forward. Each time a revolutionary idea stepped forward there arose a wild opposi-

tion until they nearly crucified the discoverer. But by some strange coincidence those discoverers were people like Pasteur who is still remembered while the condemners are forgotten. What I am trying to do is not of course as great as the really big advancements of the past but it will be one of the smaller contributions. I know that with the help of God and those few who believe as you do this will be a step into the future understanding of the human race. I wonder where there are more who will join us in this struggle.

As you know I have been avoiding publicity. I find now that this is perhaps the wrong approach for now I shall seek publicity so that Christine will become such an average thing in the minds of the public that when the next Christine comes along the public will consider it an old story and the sensation will be decreased. It's been a tough struggle thus far but it will continue and I am ready to face constantly. My emotions have leveled off at a point where I no longer shy away from people.

I am anxious to see you again. . . . Write when you get a chance. I just received a copy of the first Kinsey report, autographed by the three authors. I cherish it.

Christine

Thus began an alliance between Christine Jorgensen and Harry Benjamin that spanned several decades and touched countless lives. On July 14, 1954, Dr. William Barbarito of Jersey City performed vaginoplasty on Christine Jorgensen, with Dr. Benjamin present:

Dear Doctor Benjamin,

I wish to thank you for sending me your reprint on "Transsexuals and Transvestism."

For me to express a judgment may seem professionally

*presumptuous; however, it pleased me that my concept
to you at the hospital that fixation of ideas and drives
were based upon genetic, environmental factors or both,
was an over-simplification but nevertheless was basically
in harmony with your concept. . . .*

*Let me also say at this time I was very happy you were
present at the operation upon our mutual patient "C. J."
Also I know you are interested in knowing that thus far
the post-operative course has been satisfactory. The critical aspect mechanically in the future seems to be mostly
one of orificial diameter and depth, this I believe will be
accomplished by persistent dilatation and really is in her
hands. Another aspect which time will reveal is the
behavior of the grafts, thus far, very good.*

With personal regards,

Yours very truly

William N. Barbarito, M.D.

Due to the enormous publicity arising from the Jorgensen
phenomenon, requests for genital surgeries were escalating.
This proved a problem not only for Harry Benjamin and
Christine Jorgensen, who received most of these requests, but
for the Danish government as well. The following article
appeared in *Science Digest* in January of 1959:

> The doctors who converted the sex of ex-GI George
> Jorgensen to Christine Jorgensen have done four more
> such operations, the last within the year. Two men were in
> their forties. One was married. All were Danish.
>
> The Danish government will no longer permit surgery
> of foreigners. The widespread publicity given the Christine
> case is responsible for the decision.
>
> Since the Christine operation, the doctors have received
> about 2,000 letters from all over the world. About twen-
> ty-five per cent have come from the U.S. from individuals
> with assorted sex problems.

While the doctors at times regret the Christine operation because of the widespread publicity, they believe there has been a favorable side too. It has helped focus attention on the problem of transvestism, the desire to appear in clothes of the opposite sex.

These persons truly feel themselves a female personality in a male body. They have a pronounced desire not only to identify themselves with the feminine sex in clothing, but also by taking on a woman's name and occupying themselves with feminine tasks. To live as a male gives them mental stress and sometimes leads to suicidal attempts. Psychiatric treatment has not proved helpful and the use of hormones gives only temporary benefit.

In 1976, Harry Benjamin sent this final note to Christine Jorgensen:

My dear Chris,

Gretchen and I send you many thanks for your lovely note and wish you the very best for whatever you will undertake in the New Year.

I am happy you are well and ambitious. Unfortunately, I cannot say the same of me. At 91, I have all kinds of complaints that interfere with practically all my activities, especially reading and writing, but there is still hope for the eyes that an operation will eventually be feasible and restore enough of my eyesight so that I can read again.

We think and talk of you often. You are our queen and I hope you will remain the queen for a long time to come.

My warmest and affectionate greetings and a kiss to you, Christine.

Always your friend,

Harry

The "Christine operation" shocked the world, and generated dilemmas and controversies in psychiatry, medicine, and law, that persist half a century later. But above all, it gave hope and inspiration to many that perhaps anatomy was not destiny after all.

How Prevalent Is the Condition and Who Is Affected?

I was three or perhaps four years old when I realized that I had been born into the wrong body, and should really be a girl. I remember the moment well and it is the earliest memory of my life. . . . By every standard of logic I was patently a boy — Jan Morris, *Conundrum*

The formation of identity is a complex developmental process of progressive and regressive intrapsychic phenomenological components. Contemporary critics of sex reassignment insist that the transsexual identity emerged in response to available surgical procedures. They hold that, like the proverbial "tail that wags the dog," transsexuals did not define themselves as such prior to the existence of technological interventions. It is well known that language plays a large role in identity consolidation. Therefore, it is important to note that, even in the absence of nosology or the terminology Benjamin generated, certain individuals disclosed information that revealed a self-defined, self-proclaimed cross-gender identity that undeniably predated conversion possibilities.

Schaefer and Wheeler (1995) reviewed Harry Benjamin's first ten cases, which spanned the years 1938 to 1953. It is of historic and clinical import to retrospectively analyze how these early patients described themselves—without any commonality of language or any published information—and each of course presuming, as many patients still do today, that they are the only person in the world to have such feelings, confusion, and conflict. The value of this collective overview is twofold: First, it refutes the criticism that the transsexual is a Frankenstein created by misguided surgeons, and secondly, it yields valuable demographic information about the condition of gender dysphoria.

Benjamin's first ten patients were a heterogeneous group with varied life patterns and backgrounds. Nine were natal males and one was a natal female. Most were middle class, although three were from the upper class, according to socioeconomic barometers. The occupations of the group were also quite varied. The group consisted of a writer, an office worker, a farmer, an interior decorator, a housewife, a machinist, an entertainer, a military career person, an art student, a chemist, and a photographer. Many had been married, some more than once. Among the ten patients, three had children and one had grandchildren (Schaefer & Wheeler, 1995).

The sibling order among the first ten patients was varied, as were their phenotypes. Some reported being homosexual, some bisexual, and the remainder described themselves as heterosexual. While the intensity of the feelings of gender dysphoria varied, all ten had a history of cross-dressing from early ages into adult life.

Clinicians who have worked extensively with gender-variant clients will immediately recognize how illustrative these first ten patients are of the many diversities that exist among transgendered persons. For within this first, self-referred group of courageous people who sought assistance, many of the same issues arose that arise today. There was the true cross-dresser, the transsexual who does not desire surgery, the transsexual who requires genital reassignment surgery, the desperate self-mutilator, the very public transsexual (Christine Jorgensen) and the very private, the person whose family is understanding, and the person with the rejecting family. There are those who remained with original spouses, and those who were abandoned by spouses. There were also those whose gender condition was coexistent with a psychiatric condition. In short, these ten patients formed a microcosm of gender dysphoria.

• • •

It is extremely difficult to accurately assess the incidence and prevalence of gender-variant persons in the United States and the world at large, although there have been many attempts to do so, as the following examples illustrate.

The incidence and sex ratio of transsexualism in Sweden were calculated during the period between 1972 and 1992, using a case register at the Swedish Bureau of Social Welfare. This study was unique, in that the authors performed a similar, previous study in the 1960s and could therefore reliably compare data. The results show that the incidence figures remain constant over time and that the incidence of transsexualism is equal in men and women. The authors note that a larger group, consisting of all people who had applied for sex reassignment, revealed a preponderance of men. This larger group apparently was composed not only of transsexuals but also of what the authors consider "effeminate homosexuals, transvestites, and diagnostically uncertain cases" (Landen, Walinder, & Lundstrom, 1996).

A 1993 study in the Netherlands estimated prevalence of transsexualism by tabulating all the patients who were diagnosed as transsexuals by psychiatrists or psychologists and treated hormonally or surgically. Calculated thusly, the prevalence for male-to-female transsexualism is 1:11,900 and for female-to-male transsexuals 1:30,400 (van-Kesteren, Gooren, & Megens, 1996). The sex ratio is about 2.5 men to 1 woman. This is a higher prevalence than reported in other areas, which the authors ascribe to the "benevolent climate for the treatment of transsexualism in the Netherlands" (Bakker, van Kesteren, Gooren, & Bezemer, 1993).

Prevalence of transsexualism in Singapore was similarly

assessed by counting patients who sought sex reassignment and were diagnosed as transsexuals. Up to 1986, there were a total of 458 Singapore-born transsexuals, 343 males and 115 females. This translates to a prevalence ratio of 1:2,900 for male-to-female transsexualism and 1:8,300 for female-to-male transsexualism. The sex ratio in this study is 3 males to 1 female. Again, the high prevalence rate was attributed to the availability of sex-reassignment surgery (Tsoi, 1988).

In Germany, the ten-year period of 1981–1990 saw between 2.1 and 2.4 applications for legal sex change status per 100,000 adults, and the ratio favored male-to-female transsexuals 2.3:1 (Wietze & Osburg, 1996).

A 1997 French study of prevalence estimates the ratio of transsexualism as anywhere from 1:50,000 to 1:100,000 (Gallarda et al.,1997; Soutoul, Touze, & Froge, 1986). In 1968, Pauly estimated that the incidence of transsexuals in the United States was 1:100,000 and 1:400,000, for males and females, respectively. Ten years later, as more gender clinics appeared, estimates of incidence doubled (Belli, 1978).

While most studies document transsexualism as appearing, on average, three times as often in natal males as in females, a 1988 study in Poland obtained reversed results, with a ratio of 5.5:1, the majority being natal females (Godlewski, 1988). Similarly, the overwhelming majority of individuals who applied for sex reassignment procedures in Turkey between 1987 and 1994 were female-to-male transsexuals (Yuksel, Sahin, Karali, & Baral, 1995).

A review of the literature on prevalence of transsexualism reveals that the phenomenon is far more frequently reported in North America and Northern Europe than in third world and socialist countries or in the Mediterranean basin. Obviously, legal obstacles and societal factors greatly influence the number of transsexuals presenting as patients (Ross, Walinder, & Lundstrom,1981).

In Southeast Asia cases of gender dysphoria receive little attention, particularly among Hindus and Buddhists. Although there are numerous cases, they are of little concern to those affected or their families. This is because the condition is thought to be a residual manifestation of a previous life as a member of the opposite sex. In these cultures many persons with gender conditions claim to remember particulars of the previous life (Stevenson, 1977).

No studies about transsexualism appear concerning mainland China, as communication about sexual phenomena in China is reportedly heavily censored. However, Ruan detailed contact with seven transsexuals in China and acknowledged one case of transsexual surgery performed in China that went unpublicized (Ruan, Bullough, & Tsai, 1989).

A successful case of male-to-female surgery was implemented in East Africa. The patient was followed for years and considered to be living "a normal life as a female" (Ndirangu, 1993).

Similarly, one case of sex reassignment surgery in Hungary is reported in the literature. After psychological, gynecological, urological, and forensic consultations, two surgeons were granted legal license by the Hungarian Medical Research Council to perform surgery. The patient reported very high levels of satisfaction at a two-year follow-up (Lampe & Szokoly, 1997).

In Japan, the nation's first legal sex reassignment was scheduled to take place in 1998. Of the two hundred people who had to that point submitted requests for reassignment in Japan, 70% were biological females. It has been estimated that between 2,200 to 7,000 Japanese citizens desire sex reassignment.

It is clear, upon review, that the criteria by which researchers define *transsexualism* combine with other diagnostic and linguistic problems to obfuscate epidemiological data. All of the previous cited studies are limited to taking a "head count" of transsexuals or persons applying for reassignment procedures. None of these studies, however, addresses the more difficult issue of assessing the incidence and prevalence of gender variance, which exists on a continuum, with transsexualism at one extreme. That leaves unanswered the question of how many people are gender dysphoric but do not qualify for or desire medical procedures. The whole spectrum of such people is now more appropriately referred to by the term *transgendered*. In the United States, private practitioners of psychology and psychiatry see as many, if not more, individuals who are transgendered than gender clinics per se, yet those numbers are not included in incidence reports in the literature. Certainly, the prevalence of gender dysphoria is grossly underreported.

A conservative estimate is that 3–5% of the United States population has some degree of gender dysphoria. Others claim that 8–10% is more precise. According to a report in *Playboy* magazine, 25% of 5,000 men who responded to a survey in Britain said they cross-dressed at some time in their lives, and 8% reported doing it at least once a week. Obviously, it is virtually impossible to anchor prevalence rates to behavior that is not only private but often viewed with shame. How can we begin to query individuals about an area of behavior that is shrouded in guilt and secrecy?

Even individuals who do not attempt to hide their cross-gender behaviors may not desire or require professional interventions and, therefore, never come to the attention of caregivers. For example, many female-to-male transgendered persons are able to wear sweatshirts and jeans, sport short hair, and look mannish, without being labeled as transsexual. These people assimilate into society and go "uncounted' in surveys of gender clinics or other professional settings (Eyler & Wright, 1995). Or take the example of the cross-dresser who wears his wife's clothes when she is at work. One can begin to see the futility of estimating what is clearly a widespread yet underreported phenomenon.

If there is uncertainty about how many are affected by gen

der conditions, there is no uncertainty about who is affected. Transgendered people inhabit every nation of the world, come from all walks of life, and occupy all socioeconomic strata. Gender conditions do not discriminate on the basis of race or religion. They appear to be distributed randomly throughout the world's population, much like random birth errors. Even societies that forbid sex reassignment, such as the Islamic nations and Portugal, have had their citizens come across continents to secure much-needed treatments (Costa-Santos & Madeira, 1996).

–4–
Early Therapeutic Strategies

Irrespective of my external presentation, outside divine intervention, I will never be a man. I lack the most important ingredient, a male identity. . . . This lack of a male self-perception was not by choice, for my attempts at rectifying this situation as a young adult were honorable . . . if there existed a medication to provide concordance with my male phenotype, it would be readily accepted. Unfortunately, no such treatment exists and it is my understanding . . . that the window to alter such an identity has expired long hence. Thus, if ever there existed a branch of life as a male it has long since been pruned. — A transsexual psychiatrist

In the years following Christine Jorgensen's brave disclosure and the subsequent publication of Harry Benjamin's work, many individuals sought treatment, hoping to receive compassionate care and assistance with gender reassignment.

In 1966, Johns Hopkins became the first U.S. hospital to officially support sex-change operations (Pauly & Edgerton, 1986). By 1979, twenty major medical centers across the nation offered counseling, hormonal regimens, and operations to patients they deemed appropriate candidates for these procedures.

The same year that Hopkins began its pioneer treatment program, 1966, saw an Argentinean surgeon convicted of assault for performing a sex-change operation. Another Argentinean surgeon was also charged with aggravated assault for performing three such surgeries but later was acquitted on the technicality that all of the patients were actually pseudohermaphrodites and received "sexual clarification," not sex change (Belli, 1978).

Twenty-five years after Christine Jorgensen's transformation, sex-reassignment surgery had become a modern reality. But transsexual surgery provoked pejorative reactions from legal and medical disciplines, which clung tenaciously to the fundamental, couplet assumptions that there are two, and only two sexes, and that one's God-given sex is immutable.

Derivative of these assumptions was the evolution of legal and medical arguments that perhaps subjective states of gender could not be ethically treated by physical manipulations. Transsexualism, paradoxically, was the only condition known where the patient essentially diagnosed his own problem and went on to prescribe the treatment as well. Moreover, many doctors felt that the very desire for a sex change was symptomatic of serious psychopathology. Following this line of reasoning, the surgeon, then, was in effect removing healthy organs on the demand of a delusional patient.

A 1978 article in the *Journal of the American Medical Association* stated that "most gender clinics report that many applicants for surgery are actually sociopaths seeking notoriety, masochistic homosexuals, or borderline psychotics, and not true transsexuals" (Belli). The dilemma for medicine and law was whether voluntary transsexual surgery was lawful medicine or criminal mayhem. Mayhem statutes prohibit any act that "unlawfully and maliciously deprives a human being of a member of his body, or disables, disfigures, or renders it useless" (Belli, 1978). Less than 10% of the patients who attended the gender clinic programs received sex-reassignment surgeries. While no American surgeon had been prosecuted for mayhem because of transsexual surgery, in 1978 a New York court called the operation "an experimental form of psychotherapy by which mutilating surgery is conducted on a person with the intent of setting his mind at ease" (Belli, 1978).

While in Argentina performing the surgery was a punishable offense, other countries, including Belgium, Canada, Switzerland, and Great Britain, allowed said surgeries, if they were therapeutic and performed by a skilled practitioner. The Netherlands legitimized the surgery but required a medical-legal council to ordain approval. The surgery was unlawful in Germany (Belli, 1978).

The criterion that many countries set forth, that the surgery must be *therapeutic,* posed the most difficulties for the U.S. medical and legal communities. The question became, of course, how to determine therapeutic value. According to attorney Melvin Belli, scientists and courts were unable to concur what constitutes therapeutic benefit (1978). Should it be the surgeon's avowal that an operation was performed successfully, or did the decision rest solely on the subjective opinion of the patient? Following this theoretical trajectory longitudinally gave rise to even more complex questions: What if, after some period of time, the postoperative patient became depressed and committed suicide? Is this a priori evidence that the surgery was not therapeutic, and is the surgeon therefore liable?

Some commentators of jurisprudence argued that any drastic surgical procedure is unlawful unless there is a justifiable reason for it and it does not endanger healthy organs. Others argued that certain procedures, like rhinoplasty, have no objective therapeutic value but may confer lasting and significant positive changes in a person's well-being and serve to improve overall psychological functioning.

One might assume, in pondering the adjudication of medicolegal tort and criminal liability issues, that the patient's informed consent would be a better defense than that of therapeutic benefit. How could a surgeon be charged with malicious actions if a patient consented to them? Most courts hold that consent is immaterial when there is "any hurt or injury calculated to interfere with the health or comfort of the victim." But the real obstacle to consent preventing civil or criminal liability of the surgeon is the question of whether or not a transsexual's consent could ever be viewed as valid. So again, the issue reverts to the etiology of gender dysphoria: If transsexuals' desire to have surgery is an obsession, a delusion, or a symptom of other complex psychopathology, as many professionals believed, they are rendered mentally incompetent in the eyes of the law, and their consent lacks legal validity. Thus, law and medicine, strange bedfellows, colluded in restricting the legal rights of transsexuals and their access to treatment.

Physicians in the forefront of transsexual surgery, those who were members of the Johns Hopkins Gender Identity Team, anticipated these medical-legal challenges and formulated methods of preoperative evaluation, surgical treatment, and postoperative follow-up, thereby documenting that appropriate assessment leads to therapeutic surgeries and objective "social rehabilitation." At the Annual Meeting of the American Association of Plastic Surgeons in 1969, Edgerton, Knorr, and Callison revealed what led to the unceremonious formation of this first treatment center in a paper he presented entitled "The Surgical Treatment of Transsexual Patients: Limitations and Indications."

Edgerton had knowledge of sporadic reports of sex conversion surgeries throughout the world but, by coincidence, in 1957 he himself encountered two such patients within a matter of months. Both of these patients who presented to Edgerton had "incomplete attempts at conversion surgery." The decision to complete their partial surgeries was a far easier one to make than that of operating on someone with "unaltered genitalia." These first patients were carefully evaluated by endocrinologists, psychiatrists, and a psychologist. One was approved for surgery and the other, owing to an I.Q. of 80, was not. At approximately the same time, Dr. Howard Jones, in the department of gynecology, was being sought out by patients requesting similar surgeries. The two physicians decided to pool their experiences in the treatment of these unusual and complex situations. Thus, the Gender Identity Clinic was formally launched. At that time the team consisted of three psychiatrists, two psychologists, five surgeons, one endocrinologist, support staff, and genetic and legal consultants. The team had treated twenty-four patients surgically.

Evaluation of patients for surgery included a careful consideration of four significant parameters. The first was whether the patient was authentically motivated for surgery. Even if a patient reported a cross-gender identification from early childhood, the team must ascertain that he or she was clearly differentiated diagnostically from homosexuals, as the condition of gender conflict precedes the development of genital sexuality (Edgerton, Knorr, & Callison, 1969). Patients must have no ambivalence about surgery, and the evaluation must conclusively determine that the patient's request for surgery was not the result of a life crisis, such as a homosexual who became depressed following the loss of a lover.

Secondly, Edgerton's team addressed the question most perplexing from a legal standpoint: Is any patient who seeks surgical castration, by definition a psychotic? He concluded, on the basis of the team's evaluations, that the vast majority of transsexual patients, and certainly those who were approved for surgery, had no thought disorders. He did state, however, that schizophrenic illness occurred more often in transsexuals than in the general population, and that this was suggestive of an association between the two "disorders."

Thirdly, the question whether these patients weren't better served by psychotherapy than surgery was rhetorically addressed. The answer was that transsexual patients were not motivated to engage in psychotherapy, "as their adopted gender

34

role is strikingly ego-syntonic." Their goal was sexual reassignment, not conformation to their anatomic gender.

Finally, a careful analysis of individual patients must include a thoughtful prediction of how the patient would adjust to the experience of living in the preferred gender. There was some evidence that transsexuals who did not attempt a trial period of living in the new role before having surgery in a foreign country were thrown into "sociocultural" crises upon return. They experienced anxiety and depression generated by the inaccessibility of their past and the uncertainty of their future.

In summary, Edgerton counseled his colleagues about the role that plastic surgeons could play in surgical intervention with this population. After all, plastic surgeons were quite comfortable making alterations of the body to help achieve emotional adjustment. Transsexual patients were a more extreme case of conflict between body-image and self-identification. He cautioned plastic surgeons interested in working with these patients to organize a team approach to evaluate, diagnose, and guide the patients through the various surgical procedures, which he felt were getting progressively better, in construction of both male and female genitalia. Perhaps the most important advice he offered his fellow surgeons was the following exhortation:

> It is not difficult for the surgeon to establish a good relationship with transsexual patients—but to do so, he must deal with the patient as a member of the psychological sex chosen by the patient! To think of a male transsexual as a "male" is to completely defeat the working doctor-patient relationship. (p. 44)

About the same time that Dr. Edgerton enlightened plastic surgeons as to the surgical conversions that were being undertaken at Hopkins, a psychoanalyst, Charles Socarides, presented "A Psychoanalytic Study of the Desire for Sexual Transformation [Transsexualism]: The Plaster-of-Paris Man" to the American Psychoanalytic Association. This paper was subsequently published in *The International Journal of Psycho-Analysis.* In this presentation Socarides asserted that he had amassed substantial clinical data in treating homosexuals, transvestites, and transsexuals, and that the particular case study that he proffered would yield important psychodynamic findings to help resolve the controversies surrounding transsexualism. Socarides' position was that the transsexual is a sexual pervert who escapes homosexuality and "fastens to the idea of changing his sex through the psychotic mechanism of denial" (1970). He wrote, "My answer to the entire question of change-of-sex surgery can be stated in one sentence, the same one published in a national magazine that asked for my assessment of this issue: Such operations are doomed to ultimate failure because they do not change the basic underlying conflict" (1969).

Thus, as more physicians from different specialties began to publish their experiences with transsexual patients, there raged a debate between those in medicine who believed that the condition was a legitimate entity and those who viewed it as psychosis propagated to medical tragedy, with the surgeon as midwife.

When his psychoanalytic tenets were challenged as incorrect notions based on errors of fact and logic, the confusion of homosexuality, transvestism, and transsexualism, as well as sheer moralistic posturing, Socarides responded to his critics by publishing a letter that "conveys the pain and suffering induced by this medical tragedy far more eloquently than any attempt to rationalize such disregard of the primary injunction of medicine, primum non nocere" (Hoffman, 1969; Socarides, 1969):

> *I saw your name in the San Francisco Chronicle (where) you warn about the big mistake of trying to make women out of male nature. . . . I consider it my duty to save other human beings the agony I am living through.*

My male sexual organs are gone! Dr.---- performed "in cold blood" on me one of those horrible mutilations. My so-called artificial vagina entrance looks like a ring of empty scrotum. I will have to live, if I have the courage, with this monstrosity.

If I had seen one of those operations—Frankensteins— I would never have consented to it. Dr.---- publishes some pictures but not the essential one: a photo of the "so-called artificial vagina entrance." How can a human being do this to another? Can you imagine my situation? I will have to live with something that just gives me nausea. I paid to be crucified.

There is a transsexual movement . . . that should be stopped before more innocents, like me, get hurt . . . [and] end this awful hysteria of misfits trying to solve "a mild problem."

No surgery can possibly produce anything that . . . resembles a female vagina. . . . It needs dilatation to keep it open and if dilated too much becomes useless for intercourse. Such an open wound lacks protective membranes and bleeds under pressure. . . . A piece of phallus with an open wound below and a ring of scrotum hanging. . . . Who calls that an artificial vagina is . . . looking (for) ignorant and credulous people.

Charles Socarides' inflammatory and sensational response to his detractors unquestionably served to galvanize the opinions of those who saw surgery as mayhem. It would not be the only occasion upon which the specter of "postoperative regret" would be conjured to silence the opponents.

By late 1969 the debate was no longer limited to specialists who treated transsexual patients. The editor of *Medical World News* sent the following letter to a renowned professor of pediatrics, Dr. Robert S. Mendelsohn:

October 6, 1969

Dear Bob:

You come to mind as the guy who might help me salvage a significant story that was inadvertently crowded out of our editorial pages. It concerns the new book by Drs. Money and Green at Johns Hopkins, Transsexualism and Sex Reassignment. *For most of a year I'd been working on the J-H press to release galleys on this book as they appeared. I thought it should make news, and therefore relinquished my claim to it as a book review. Now that the book is about to be released, it appears that it was bypassed as a story . . . .*

I want to pick up the pieces by getting out a lead feature book review at the soonest date. What I need is a powerful, socially conscious writer who'll discuss it from the humane point of view. That's you, if you can be had. I'm in the act of trying to retrieve the book itself. I moved it along so fast I didn't get to examine it. But I understand that these two men have made Johns Hopkins the world center for the people who were born with (or had visited on them at birth) a confusion of gender. I'm particularly interested in Dr. Pauly's statement that the transsexual syndrome shouldn't be dismissed as merely homosexual.

At this minute, I can't seem to reach you by phone. So I decided to bash out a note to you to ask if you will be interested in seeing and commenting on this book. If you are, please phone me collect, and I'll put wings on the book . . . .

Best Regards,

Melva Weber (editor)

October 10, 1969

Dear Bob,

Sorry I missed your call . . . . I'll send the book right out. I showed it to one of our editors with a lot of background in sex studies and he says all the renowned specialists in this field are contributors to the text. Anyway, I wanted the review done by somebody who is professional and authoritative . . . . You can't escape my relentless pursuit.

Melva

In February 1970, *Medical World News* did indeed print a lead feature book review entitled, "Surgical Sex Reassignment: A Passionate Judgment." It read as follows:

> Drs. Richard Green and John Money, editors of *Transsexualism and Sex Reassignment,* present ideas and findings soberly, intellectually, and with restraint. But I progressed through its pages with a persistent, growing sense of uneasiness that culminated in a gut reaction bordering on revulsion.
>
> Why? As professionals, we are taught that our reason must rule over our passions. But as human beings, we know instinctively, as well as from history, that pure reason has often led mankind into serious error. Passion, emotion, and feelings deserve at least equal time. Doctors as well as others should approach this book and its subject area frankly and without apology, from an emotional as well as an intellectual standpoint. Even King Solomon prayed for "an informed heart."
>
> In the book, Dr. John D. Hoopes, a surgeon, admits, "When first confronted by this problem (a demand for change in gender) the male surgeon experiences mixed emotions while listening to the plea for surgery from a physically attractive young female, and while examining the breasts for the specific purpose of amputation." But he does manage to go ahead with the surgery, since it is "in keeping with the patient's quest."

Dr. Howard Jones, in the chapter "Operative Treatment of the Male Transsexual," mentions no such qualms as he removes perfectly normal penises. But I experienced a jolt from the operative illustrations, showing—in ten drawings—how to amputate a penis and construct a vagina.

The pictures of artificial apparatuses to maintain vaginal size, and of an artificially constructed phallus, deserve to be regarded from an emotional as well as an intellectual view. From me, they elicited strong feelings, ranging from queasiness to horror.

The book deals comprehensively with the historical, social, clinical, psychologic, somatic, and legal aspects of transsexuals, and presentations are of good technical quality. But there is also a good bit of self-congratulatory rhetoric. Men working in this field are referred to as "dedicated scientists who had to break through powerful barriers of superstition and prejudice" on a "medical frontier" surrounded by "emotionalism." This kind of florid prose does serve to indicate that an emotional approach is not limited to the opponents of the authors and their methods!

But the proponents of sex reassignment have every right to regard themselves as an embattled minority. In a survey made by the Johns Hopkins group, the majority of physicians polled were opposed to the surgical procedure because of the risks of medical censure and malpractice suits, and on religious and moral grounds. Indeed, 94% objected on the moral and religious basis alone. The authors comment: "This last figure was unexpected from a group frequently considered to be by reason of their professional goals, morally non-judgmental."

What a lot they have to learn about doctors! For in spite of the monasticism, isolation, and rigorousness of modern medical education, physicians still remain human beings and citizens. We should indeed rejoice that the humanism, ethics, and basic compassion of the physician still exercise such a strong influence. Our age has witnessed, in the behavior of doctors in Nazi Germany, the results of complete dependence on objective, rational science.

The essence of moral or religious law is its immunity

from popular behavior and mores at any particular point in history. Therefore, the historical and traditional factors assume great relevance to the sex reassignment question. The whole life span of the individual involved must be considered, too. Follow-up studies on these patients cover a very short period, and are fragmentary. There is an obvious need for a control group, so that the natural course of this condition can be observed and accurately described. While classic psychiatric approaches seem to offer little, either in treatment or in understanding the etiology of gender-role disorientation, other methods such as aversion treatment may be more successful. And because such treatment does not have the finality and irreversibility of surgery, the chapter on it adds greatly to the eclecticism—and consequent value—of the book.

The work of sex reassignment belongs to a large category of activities in our culture, which includes moon shots, lobotomy, and heart transplants. These achievements have two major characteristics: first, a high degree of technical capability—they can all be done, and done well. But second, they are all subject to a gnawing question: Are they worth doing at all? How many of our pursuits, accomplished with technical skill and competence, are futile?

There are serious questions whether the entire activity is proper, and if so, what priority it serves in our hierarchy of values and in the competing world of research. These are questions not to be answered by science alone, but requiring the active involvement of man qua man.

Doctors in general, and particularly psychiatrists, responded with impassioned support of this position. The following was written by one of the most renown and widely published psychiatrists of the day:

March 2, 1970
Dear Bob,
Your comments in Medical World News *on sex reassign-*

ment is certainly correct in general and is not restrained. Aside from the violation of the primary principle of doing no harm to the patient, and aside from the smug complacency of this dehumanized gang whose consciences require no more sop than doing what the patient wants, I think there is reason to distrust both their descriptions and the very existence of this "disease" called "transsexualism."

In regard to the former, Socarides in New York, published a letter from a victim, who was utterly miserable. I recently read a paper, submitted for publication, describing the wretched, hopeless existence of one of these "women." Of course, once the mutilation is done, a sober assessment of the results might lead logically to suicide. How could such a patient make an honest statement?

In regard to the latter point, this "disease" seems to have sprung up in compliance with the "advances" in surgical butchery. Who ever heard of it before these surgical geniuses made their expertise known? You may have noticed, in the book that the patients keep on trying to get more and more surgery. I suspect the whole thing is an iatrogenic matter that permits the patient to become the collaborator in a disguised, horrible, regressive representation of a sadistic sexual act.

While analysis certainly has limitations, I do not think there would be much difficulty in at least demonstrating psychotic mechanisms—if only one could get one of these surgeons as a patient.

Sincerely yours.

S.D.L., M.D.

Dr. Edgerton, founder of the Hopkins clinic responded with the following:

Dear Dr.,

Your recent "Point of View" article on sex reassignment prompts me to write you a short note. You have obviously spoken from the heart and with great thoughtfulness after reading the book by Green and Money. I, too, have gone through many of the same reactions that you have expressed. I completely agree with you that doctors and scientists must include instinct and emotion along with reason in making total judgments. As the original organizer of the Gender Identity Clinic at Hopkins, I felt it important to study dispassionately the effects of this approach on both individual humans and on the society. At the moment I am rather convinced that if I were such a patient, surgery would offer me the only existing realistic hope for happiness. It is far from an ideal solution. I continue to ask these patients if they have had second thoughts about their surgery. They do not. Quite to the contrary, they remain very grateful for the assistance. I agree that it is very important that other groups offering treatment by means of aversion treatment or by other methods, should try to find an easier and equally satisfactory solution; but it is far from certain that these patients have only an emotional disorder or one that is determined by environmental effects alone. In some respects we find that we have to weigh our own learned emotional reactions to this type of surgery against the growing body of evidence that such surgery produces great human relief for the patients.

Your opinion is much respected, and I trust you will allow me to carry on running dialogue with you about this over the next few years. I will promise to keep an open mind to the limitations of such surgery, and I hope you will find some way to perhaps interview a few of the patients who have gone through this procedure.

Warmest personal regards,

Milton T. Edgerton, M.D.

But Edgerton's proposed "running dialogue" would never leave the starting gate:

April 2, 1970

Dear Bob,

Thank you for the copy of the letter from Edgerton, but I have no interest in participating in further discussion with him. I think of the surgical procedure as a sort of perversion and crime. To ask a patient who has already had his penis and testes amputated if he has "second thoughts" is ludicrously ingenious.

That surgeons should incorporate into their competence the mutilation and destruction of avowedly normal tissue upon the indication of "happiness" is not a subject that I can "discuss."

Sincerely yours,

S.D.L.

It was within this context of polarization that other gender clinics followed the lead of the John Hopkins Gender Identity Clinic. Meanwhile, individual practitioners, particularly those who specialized in sex therapy, endocrinology, or plastic surgery, were approached by patients who presented with gender conflicts.

While certain individuals successfully navigated through the stringent demands of these clinics and nascent programs, many others were turned away, or left in frustration. Part of the inadequacy of these pioneer clinics lay in the theoretical misconstruction of the condition, misguided notions of what therapy should consist of, and the rigid criteria applied in diagnosis. For example, only primary, as opposed to secondary, transsexuals were considered eligible for reassignment procedures. Primary transsexuals are individuals who are markedly aware, from early childhood, that they are gender-discordant. They do not attempt to deny the condition or to live in the assigned gender. They do not marry, produce offspring, or exhibit the "flight into hypermasculinity" that the secondary male-to-female transsexual displays in a futile attempt to cure himself of the condition (Brown, 1988).

While the constricted diagnostic criteria of these early treatment centers excluded many persons who sought treatment, far worse was the fate of another group of gender-variant individuals: the institutionalized. Many people who sought psychiatric help for their gender condition, and the inevitable depression that resulted, were involuntarily committed. It is not uncommon to meet patients who received shock therapy or other aversive treatment during this era, often with the support of their parents, who were horrified by contrary gender expressions and feared that they were precursors to homosexuality. Many adolescents were diagnosed as "gender identity disorder in childhood" at the behest of psychiatrists who admonished parents to curb sissy or tomboy behaviors and thus "nip them in the bud" (Burke, 1996).

In the spring of 1979, Johns Hopkins Hospital stopped performing sex-reassignment surgery, following the publication of research that failed to show "objective improvements" in patients' lives. Dr. Jon K. Meyer, associate professor of psychiatry and director of the sexual behaviors consultation unit, conducted the research. Meyer said that "surgical intervention has done nothing objective beyond what time and psychotherapy can do," to improve the stability of transsexuals ("Sex-change surgery," 1979).

Meyer's study was widely cited by professionals and appeared in the popular press. Meyer was quoted as saying there were "no differences in long-term adjustment between transsexuals who go under the scalpel and those who do not" (*Time* magazine, 1979) and "My personal feeling is that surgery is not a proper treatment for this psychiatric disorder and it's clear to me that these patients have severe psychological problems that don't go away following surgery" (*New York Times*, 1979).

In 1980 Fleming, Steinman, and Bocknek mounted a challenge to the Meyer's study, citing numerous methodological and conceptual flaws in research design, score reporting, interpretation of data, and conclusions. To cite but one example, transsexuals were assigned a quantitative score of (minus 1) if they cohabited with a person of "the non-gender-appropriate sex." It is not clear from Meyer's report whether this cohabitation implied sexual intimacy or on what basis this cohabitation would be negative. This is but one example of the value judgments and researcher bias that woefully contaminated the findings.

But the concerns voiced about the Meyer study were more far-reaching than issues of operationalizing or standardizing outcome variables. The more serious concern was its impact on public perception:

> We sense a growing fear of transsexualism which has found a voice in the public press . . . . We are not asking for an end to reasonable debate but only an admittance of the value-laden nature of such investigations. We are not advocating surgical re-assignment but rather the necessity for careful investigation of its appropriateness and results . . . . researchers have a responsibility to ask themselves how their results are to be used and by whom. Even if the press has misquoted Dr. Meyer, we can't help but wonder

about his willingness in the conclusion of his article to over-generalize without seemingly being aware of its impact on the general populace. The finality with which he makes his assertion merits criticism when one realizes how much further research is necessary and how many people will use his results to treat transsexualism as a psychological problem which warrants no more attention than simply letting time heal. (Fleming et al., 1980)

Physicians play a unique and dictatorial role in the creation of societal perceptions of reality. For example, sixty years ago, childbirth was a social event. Women gave birth at home, with the help of a female midwife, and in the presence of the family. Today, childbirth is a medical event. It is treated as an illness and takes place in hospitals. This shift in the way our society views birthing has occurred because we have adopted a medical perception of childbirth.

The legal and judicial systems empower doctors to so define and codify "reality." Science and research are often left trailing behind, shadowing the obliquity of judgment of the medical authorities.

5

Etiology of Gender Dysphoria

No true transsexual has yet been persuaded, bullied, drugged, analyzed, shamed, ridiculed, or electrically shocked into an acceptance of his physique.
— Jan Morris, *Conundrum*

Owing to the intricate relationship of etiology and treatment, it is not surprising that early therapies were designed to cure people of what was considered a psychiatric disorder or, falling short of that goal, to ameliorate their discomfort.

Early hypotheses about the genesis of transsexualism pointed to environmental factors in the nature vs. nurture antipodal paradigm.

The psychoanalytic model presupposed serious object-relation disturbances and pathologically introjected, highly cathected mother-child relations (Lothstein, 1979). Those advancing this model maintained that close, retrospective observations would reveal that the adult transsexual was a child who could not separate without intense anxiety, on the part of both mother and child (Gilpin, Raza, & Gilpin, 1979; Moberly, 1986; Ovesey & Person, 1976). The difficulty lay in the patient's inability to adequately regulate the intrapsychic distance between self and others (Macvicar, 1978).

Psychoanalytic literature focused on the dynamics beneath the desire to change sex. Various mechanisms were suggested to account for transsexual wishes. While some psychoanalytically oriented professionals described the psychopathology to be of a psychotic nature (Socarides, 1978), others conceptualized a borderline personality organization. In this theoretical model, the male-to-female patient seeks to "discard bad and aggressive features and to replace them with a new, idealized perfection" (Lothstein, 1984). These analysts suggested that sex reassignment surgery could best be conceptualized as "a new type of psychosurgery" (Kavanaugh & Volkan, 1978). In the case of the female-to-male transsexual, the dynamically oriented explanation was that the need to change sex arose from the child's desire to protect mother and self from a threatening father (Bradley, 1980).

By 1982, the psychoanalytic theory of gender disorders had crystallized into the following summary position:

> Sex reassignment is a symptomatic compromise formation serving defensive and expressive functions. The symptoms are the outgrowth of developmental trauma affecting body ego and archaic sense of self caused by peculiar symbiotic and separation-individuation phase relationships. The child exists in the pathogenic (and reparative) maternal fantasy in order to repair her body image and to demonstrate the interconvertability of the sexes. . . . gender pathology bears common features with other preoedipal syndromes. Transsexualism is closely linked to perversions and the clinical syndromes may shade from one into another. However, what is kept at the symbolic level in the perversions must be made concrete in transsexualism. The clinical complaint of the transsexual is a condensation of remarkable proportions. When the transsexual says that he is a girl trapped in a man's body, he sincerely means what he says. As with other symptoms, however, it takes a long time before he begins to say what he means. (Meyer, 1982)

The successful treatment of transsexualism via psychoanalysis is claimed in the literature in scattered case studies (Haber, 1991), with analysis of a full-blown transference neurosis being viewed as the ultimate resolution (Loeb, 1992; Loeb & Shane, 1982). A literature review of the last three decades also reports one case of transsexualism having been cured through exorcism and faith healing! (Barlow, Abel, & Blanchard, 1977).

Throughout the aforementioned psychiatric literature, one finds frequent mention of the transsexual's unwillingness to engage in the psychotherapeutic process and resistance to therapeutic interventions (e.g., Shtasel, 1979). White (1997), a psychiatrist, has observed similar language invoked in early psychiatric response to patients who were diagnosed with obsessive-compulsive disorders. When analysis fails, a "blame the victim" dictum prevails.

Running parallel to the psychoanalytic theories of pathogenesis are the endeavors to find a biological basis for the condition (Buhrich, Barr, & Lam-Po-Tang, 1978). Early attempts to find an organic genesis range from roentgenological examination of the skulls of transsexuals (Lundberg, Sjovall, & Walinder, 1975) to a search for an anomalous hormonal milieu (Gooren, 1986; Kula, Dulko, Pawlikowski, Imelinski, & Slowikowska, 1986).

Some early studies, first appearing in 1979, looked promising in detecting incongruous H-Y antigen status in transsexuals (Eicher et al., 1980; Spoljar, Eicher, Eiermann, & Cleve, 1981). Through cytotoxicity assays, initial reports found H-Y antigen expression to be discordant with anatomic sex and to correspond instead to the gender identity of the transsexual (Eicher et al., 1981; Engel, Pfafflin, & Wiedeking, 1980). H-Y antigen, thought to be a presumptive inducer of the testis, is present in the cells of normal males and not in the cells of normal females. Researchers felt that these results would "help to replace emotional controversy by rational assessment of facts" (Vogel, 1981).

By 1982, Meyer-Bahlburg concluded that attempts to implicate the H-Y antigen in the etiology of the condition had failed (Wachtel et al., 1986); nevertheless, some researchers felt strongly that hormonal-dependent structural brain changes, though not yet demonstrated, seemed likely (Gooren, 1990).

Similarly failing to bear fruit were studies that documented a high rate of temporal EEG abnormalities in transsexuals. Despite early accounts of this phenomenon (Hoenig, & Kenna, 1979; Nusselt & Kockott, 1976), subsequent reports, which refuted the reliability of visual EEG analyses and utilized quantitative frequency EEG analysis, found no significant differences between transsexuals and normals (Grasser, Keidel, & Kockott, 1989). And in 1991 a study using magnetic resonance imaging ruled out differences in shape and size of the splenium of the corpus callosum as a marker of transsexualism (Emory, Williams, Cole, Amparo, & Meyer).

Clinical psychologists had a unique contribution to make in this search for causality. Through the use of psychological tests they could substantiate, or fail to substantiate, the claim that transsexuals had rampant psychopathology. Once again, findings reported in the literature could buttress either position. For example, a 1985 study hypothesized that transsexuals manifested a borderline personality organization and operationalized Kernberg's criteria for borderline personality with the use of Rorschach protocols. This study found that, compared to normals, transsexuals and borderlines display intense levels of aggression, poor object relations, poor reality testing, and impaired boundary differentiation. The author concluded that male gender dysphorics are a subgroup of borderline disorders (Murray, 1985).

Studies that looked at sex-change applicants' responses to Minnesota Multiphasic Personality Inventory testing were evenly divided in concluding that they do or do not shows signs of psychopathology (Greenberg & Laurence, 1981). Some of these differences were clarified when researchers distinguished between sex-reassignment applicants who were living as men and those who were living in their preferred female gender. The latter group showed no elevations in the clinical scales, which the authors described as a "a notable absence of psychopathology" (Greenberg & Laurence, 1981; Tsushima & Wedding, 1979). One study found length of hormonal treatment to be related to emotional adjustment on four clinical scales: scores indicating greater adjustment correlated positively with longer periods of hormonal treatment (Leavitt, Berger, Hoeppner, & Northrop, 1980).

In a well-designed research study, Cole, O'Boyle, Emory, and Meyer (1997) retrospectively examined the comorbidity between gender dysphoria and psychopathology by reviewing the charts of 435 gender dysphoric individuals (318 males and 117 females). Extensive information existed for this group, including MMPI data. They reported an absence of Axis I and Axis II diagnoses and concluded that transsexualism "is usually an isolated diagnosis and not part of any general psychopathological disorder." In other words, transsexuals did not inevitably have a coexisting psychiatric disorder, which seemed to be the operating assumption of many professionals (Bodlund, Kullgren, Sundbom, & Hojerback, 1993).

In a discussion of Dutch adolescent transsexuals who had been surgically reassigned, Cohen-Kettenis and van Goozen (1997) noted that adolescent transsexuals are psychologically healthier than adult transsexuals. This suggests that the longer an individual suffers by living unsuccessfully in his or her phenotypic role, the more vulnerable he or she is to depression ensuing from the social and emotional difficulties of trying to hide the condition. Another study of adolescent transsexuals in the Netherlands compared them to adolescent psychiatric outpatients. These authors concluded that "the argument that gross psychopatholgy is a required condition for the development of transsexualism appears indefensible" (Cohen, de Ruiter, Ringelberg, & Cohen-Kettenis, 1997).

As more and more people came forth requesting treatment

and medical resources, interested investigators began to compile substantial data about the medical and psychological histories of these individuals. While the histories were consistent, in that all of these individuals had suffered similar distress, there was no commonality in terms of environmental features or in any of the particulars of their biographical data. Some reported unhappy childhoods and broken homes or blatantly dysfunctional families, while others were born to privilege or claimed to have had happy childhoods (Buhrich & McConaghy, 1978). Few of the population were sexually abused, as some theorists had speculated, and there were no similarities in terms of birth order, sexual experiences in childhood, or child-rearing practices of the parents. In short, there was no empirical evidence that environmental factors alone could account for the origin of the condition.

Interestingly, the most compelling clues as to the origin of the condition came from a seemingly unrelated group of people: baby girls who were born with adrenogenital syndrome. In this syndrome, baby girls are born without an important enzyme necessary for the making of an adrenal hormone called cortisol. They have mixed genitalia, which include an oversized clitoris that resembles a penis. Left untreated, at four years of age their appearance will begin to show signs of masculinity.

Treatment for this condition became available in the 1950s. It consists of administering corticosteroids from birth on and surgically correcting the appearance of the genitals so that they become decidedly female. With this treatment, these babies are indistinguishable from other infant girls. But as they mature, they show behavior more typical of boys than girls (Zucker et al., 1996). Longitudinal studies of these children found them to be tomboys, and as they grew, they all remarked that they would have preferred to have been male. This paralleled the transsexual experience and cast further doubt on the nurture component of the nature vs. nurture controversy.

If it is indeed true that there is a biological etiology of transsexualism, it is based on the belief that gender identity derives from hormone-induced cephalic differentiation at some critical gestational stage (Dorner, Poppe, Stahl, Kolzsch, & Uebelhack, 1991; Elias & Valenta, 1992; Giordano & Giusti, 1995). A derivative designed to test this belief would be to determine if any phenotypic differences separate the transsexual population from the general population. A 1992 report published in the *Journal of the American Medical Association* documented that three times as many male-to-female transsexuals were left-handed, compared to the general population (Watson & Coren, 1992). In a 1996 study that looked at height as a phenotypic variable, Ettner, Schacht, Brown, Niederberger, and Schrang demonstrated that the male transsexual population tends to be of greater than average height.

Looking at pathophysiology of the female-to-male transsexual, van-Straalen, Hage, and Bloemena (1995) used histological investigation to conclude that an anomalous inframammary ligament extending from the sternum to the lateral margin of the pectoralis major muscle is present in female-to-male transsexuals. Several studies have documented a higher rate of polycystic ovaries in this population (Bosinski et al., 1997a; Futterweit, 1983; Futterweit & Deligdisch, 1986; Futterweit & Krieger, 1979; Futterweit, Weiss, & Fagerstrom, 1986; Spinder, Spijkstra, Gooren, & Burger, 1989).

Bosinski et al. (1997b) examined the relationship between body build, androgens, and female-to-male transsexualism. They assessed anthropometric measurements in hormonally untreated female-to-males in comparison to healthy female and male controls. The female-to-male group differed from control females on seven of fourteen sex-dimorphic indices of masculinity/femininity in body build. The transsexuals were more masculine in body shape, primarily in bone proportion and fat distribution. Levels of testosterone and androstenedione were significantly higher in the female-to-males than in the control females. Unbound testosterone was also higher in female-to-males than in control females, and correlated positively with masculine body configuration.

White has theorized that "neuronal pruning" may be the process responsible for normal gender identity development as well as transsexualism—a common final pathway encompassing varying degrees of nature and nurture. It is assumed that gender identity is a process that begins in utero and is consolidated by three years of age. White suggests that the fetal brain is primed for gender identity development by an anatomic "sculpting" of location. This location is impacted by an active pruning of neurons during the third trimester of fetal life. The mechanisms involved in gender identity consolidation may follow patterns similar to those of other developmental processes, such as language acquisition:

> The neural proliferation within the neural tube undergoes a caudal migration ending between weeks 18 to 24. Over half of the neurons and glial cells generated undergo an active pruning process—a programmed cell death known as apoptosis. Genes become activated to prune specific brain cells and once pruned they cannot regenerate. Activation of these cellular "suicide" genes involves genetic, hormonal, and immunologic factors, although chance may also play a role.
>
> It has been shown that the right hemisphere develops approximately ten days before the left. In most individuals, there is an active pruning of the right hemisphere such that when the left hemisphere develops it claims dominance. If this active pruning on the right does not occur; and if this involves the motor strip of the brain, the right hemisphere may attain dominance resulting in a left-handed individual. If this process involves the language center, the result may be dyslexia. Since testosterone is involved in cell survival, it potentially can effect pruning and thus may account for the increased rates of dyslexia in boys. If this

same process involves the area in the brain wherein lies one's sense of gender identity (one promising possibility is the central subdivision of the bed nucleus of the stria terminalis [BSTc] in the hypothalamus noted by Zhou et al., 1995, to be a sexually dimorphic nucleus), then it could potentially result in a discordant gender identity. In some manner that is poorly understood, within the structural components of the brain, within these connections of neurons and synapses, lies one's core sense of gender self. As with any developmental process, the route taken may be quite different than expected. Neurons, too, can take the "road less traveled."

Yet neurons are only one piece of the equation and the potential etiologic factors span from neuronal migration to synaptic pruning, the latter being mainly a postnatal phenomenon. Differentiation of the primary sexual features occurs during approximately the third month of uterine life. At this stage of development, the neurons are undergoing a rapid proliferation and migration. Testosterone not only serves as the key ingredient propagating primary sexual development in the normal male but may also differentiate brain development through modulation of either the migration or pruning process. Whether via a receptor defect, inadequate hormonal levels, or genetic abnormalities of migration or pruning, the brain region responsible for gender identity may be either predisposed or set to a specific gender identity. In light of the developmental processes at this time, this period is certainly worthy of consideration in exploring the etiologic cascade.

If gender identity consolidation relies heavily on nurture, then synaptic pruning within an epigenetic framework is an etiologic candidate. Synaptogenesis, or the creation of synapses, begins during the second trimester and is most rapid during the first year of life—although this is somewhat dependent on the region of the brain. As with neurons, the synapses also undergo an active pruning process that correlates with a decline in brain plasticity. Since synaptic activity accounts for approximately fifty percent of this pruning process, it is feasible that certain environmental triggers could augment a discordant gender identity—most probably in the context of an underlying predisposition. Nurture can modulate nature through mechanisms such as immediate-early genes. Whichever pathway, be it migration, neuronal genesis, or pruning and/or synaptogenesis or pruning, gender identity becomes fixed over time with the decrement of brain plasticity. Once crystallized, it becomes as difficult to change as forgetting one's mother tongue. (1997)

With sophisticated new technologies, such as functional magnetic resonance imaging and positron emission tomography, brain activity and structure can be envisaged as never before. At present, there is a rapidly mounting assemblage of brain structure research. These studies reveal differences in the structure and function of female and male brains. Zhou, Hofman, Gooren, and Swaab at the Netherlands Institute for Brain Research in Amsterdam broke new ground in announcing, in 1995, that there exists a detectable difference in transsexual brains, as viewed at autopsy.

The specific region under study is the area of the bed nucleus of the stria terminals, BSTc, an area essential for sexual behavior. The autopsied brains revealed that the genetically male transsexuals had a female brain structure, for the volume of the central sulcus of the stria terminalis of the hypothalamus was similar in male-to-female transsexuals and genetic females. Heterosexual and homosexual males displayed a larger volume. This supports the hypothesis that gender identity develops as an interactive affair between the brain and sex hormones.

This research has had an enormous impact. Some European laws have been changed to reflect this new recognition that transsexuals are born, not made, and as such deserve medical care and legal protection. We in the United States have not followed suit, as yet.

An unfortunate surgical accident and its widely reported consequences seemed to buttress this view of gender identity as existing independent of gonadal and anatomical sex. In 1973, researchers at Johns Hopkins University published the case of an infant male twin whose penis was injured, and then amputated. The child was reared as a girl, and the case seemed to offer proof that infants are genderless at birth and that the process of socialization establishes gender identity.

But in 1997, Milton Diamond and H. Keith Sigmundson presented a long-term follow-up of this highly publicized case that sharply contradicted the alleged success of this child's reassignment to a female gender. The patient, who was raised as a girl, knew nothing of the accident that occurred at birth, and though given female hormones, steadfastly maintained a male identity. "Joan" as the infant was named, would tear off her dresses and reject dolls, and consistently preferred male companions. She rebuked her mother's attempts to have her wear makeup and tried to urinate standing. As she entered puberty and grew breasts, she stopped taking the female hormones because she so disliked the changes that were occurring. At that point she was suicidal. At age 14, still unaware of her past, she refused to continue life as a girl. Her father broke down and revealed the surgical accident, the subsequent removal of the testes, and the creation of the neovagina. This information proved to be a great relief to Joan. For the first time, life made sense. Joan requested male hormones, had mastectomy, and began phalloplasty to try to regain a male anatomy. At 25, "John" married. Even though the reassignment surgeries were only moderately successful, John was happier than ever before.

In a second documented case of a boy similarly reared as a girl after the genitals were damaged during circumcision, the outcome was unlike that described above. In this newly publicized case, the reassigned child adapted to a female identity, lives as a woman, and describes herself as bisexual ("Manipulating Gender," 1998). In the first case the reassignment took place at twenty-one months, whereas in the second case surgery was performed at seven months. These cases suggest that, while gender identity is not solely a result of socialization, there appears to be a critical period—a window of time after birth—during which gender identity consolidates.

6

Diagnostic Considerations

*Should the question of a person's identity be limited by
the results of mere histological section or biochemical
analysis with a complete disregard for the human brain,
the organ responsible for most functions and reactions,
many so exquisite in nature, including sex orientation?
I think not.* — Judge Pecora, *In Anonymous*

Male-to-Female Issues

Only a certain percentage of individuals who disclose gender
dysphoric feelings express a desire or intention to live full-time
in the preferred gender. Many wish to maintain a partial or
intermittent cross-gender presentation, or to live in an androgynous state. While some want and need medical interventions,
many want or need only social or psychological interventions.

Clinicians can help clients determine where they lie on the
continuum of gender dysphoria. Many professionals have little
knowledge about the nature of cross-dressing behaviors and
assume they are entirely fetishistic in nature. While paraphilias
are occasionally present in this population, they are the exception and not the rule. Therefore, responsible diagnostic evaluation presupposes that the clinician thoroughly understand the
difference between sex and gender.

Additionally, one must not confuse gender roles with gender
identity (Money, 1994b). An individual can easily adopt the
roles and behavior typically associated with the opposite gender without feeling as though he or she is of the opposite gender. We have witnessed a great loosening of the restrictions in

gender roles, as evidenced in the "Mister Mom" scenario, but this has no direct bearing on the condition of gender dysphoria. In other words, the stay-at-home dad may display behaviors consistent with the traditionally ascribed gender role of the female, without believing that his innermost self is female or wanting to make a gender transition.

To further complicate an area of inquiry already besieged by inconsistencies of definitions, labels, and constructs, the notion of to whom the transgendered individual is attracted must be clarified. In the past, researchers have discussed the attraction to a sexual partner as either homosexual or heterosexual, with the biological genitals of the gender patient as the referent (Blanchard,1985; Freund, Steiner, & Chan, 1982). That is to say, a male-to-female transsexual who had sexual activity with a male was considered to be homosexual, according to most writers. One must bear in mind that this identification may prove offensive to the transgendered person. Sexuality can rarely be reduced to mere genital contact; it is, rather, an admixture of affectional, emotional, and erotic components that can and do exist in many forms over the period of a lifetime. A transgendered individual, like the non-transgendered, can be heterosexual, homosexual, bisexual, or asexual (Bockting & Coleman, 1992; Schaefer, 1995). Bockting and Coleman (1992) advocated that sexual orientation be separated from gender identity and regarded it as an "unnecessary distraction" in diagnosis. They cautioned against restricting sex-reassignment procedures to those who "conform to a heterosexist paradigm of mental health" (p 149).

The *DSM-IV* criteria for making diagnoses are listed in Table 6.1. It should be pointed out that many members of the transgendered community oppose the inclusion of gender conditions in the *DSM-IV,* believing that this serves only to stigmatize individuals. These criteria are used for both male-to-female and female-to-male individuals.

Table 6.1
DSM-IV Diagnostic Criteria for Gender Identity Disorder

A. A strong and persistent cross-gender identification (not merely a desire for any perceived cultural advantages of being the other sex).

In children, the disturbance is manifested by four (or more) of the following:

(1) repeatedly stated desire to be, or insistence that he or she is, the other sex

(2) in boys, preference for cross-dressing or simulating female attire: in girls, insistence on wearing only stereotypical masculine clothing

(3) strong and persistent preferences for cross-sex roles in make-believe play or persistent fantasies of being the other sex

(4) intense desire to participate in the stereotypical games and pastimes of the other sex

(5) strong preference for playmates of the other sex

In adolescents and adults, the disturbance is manifested by symptoms such as a stated desire to be the other sex, frequent passing as the other sex, desire to live or be treated as the other sex, or the conviction that he or she has the typical feelings and reactions of the other sex.

B. Persistent discomfort with his or her sex or sense of inappropriateness in the gender role of that sex.

In children, the disturbance is manifested by any of the following: in boys, assertion that his penis or testes are disgusting or will disappear or the assertion that it would be better not to have a penis or aversion toward rough-and-tumble play and rejection of male stereotypical toys, games, and activities; in girls, rejection of urinating in a sitting position, assertion that she has or will grow a penis, or assertion that she does not want to grow breasts or menstruate or marked aversion toward normative feminine clothing.

In adolescents and adults, the disturbance is manifested by symptoms such as preoccupation with getting rid of primary and secondary sex characteristics (e.g., request for hormones, surgery, or other procedures to physically alter sexual characteristics to simulate the other sex) or belief that he or she was born the wrong sex.

C. The disturbance is not concurrent with a physical intersex condition.
D. The disturbance causes clinically significant distress or impairment in social, occupational, or other important areas of functioning.

Code based on current age:

302.6 Gender Identity Disorder in Children
302.85 Gender Identity Disorder in Adolescents or Adults

Specify if (for sexually mature individuals):

Sexually Attracted to Males
Sexually Attracted to Females
Sexually Attracted to Both
Sexually Attracted to Neither (pp. 537-8)

The *DSM-IV* identifies transvestic fethishism, a paraphilia, as a sexual disorder. It is distinct from the gender identity disorders. The diagnostic criteria are listed in Table 6.2.

Table 6.2
DSM-IV Diagnostic Criteria for Transvestic Fetishism

A. Over a period of at least 6 months, in a heterosexual male, recurrent intense sexually arousing fantasies, sexual urges, or behaviors involving cross-dressing.
B. The fantasies, sexual urges, or behaviors cause clinically significant distress or impairment in social, occupational, or other important areas of functioning.

Specify if:
With Gender Dysphoria: if the person has persistent discomfort with gender role or identity (p. 531)

The clinician who treats gender-variant clients will eventually come to appreciate the range and variation of expressions of gender conditions. Among transgendered people there seems to be a high predominance of cross-dressers. Many of these individuals will experience crises at various times in their lives and may even appear transsexual, stating a desire to transition or live full-time in the preferred role. For some, this escalation of dysphoria may coincide with traumatic life events and then wane when the trauma resolves. For others, however, there may have been an initial denial of the severity and persistence of gender dysphoria, along with false self-labeling as "cross-dresser," until some critical point, when they confront their prolonged discomfort with their anatomic sex.

Often, the histories of cross-dressers and transsexuals are similar (Levine, 1993). Many individuals had periods of fetishistic sexual behavior and cross-dressing at puberty, which shifted to cross-dressing without sexual arousal and gender dysphoria. In fact, some researchers have claimed that cross-gender fetishistic behavior or cross-dressing always precede transsexualism (Hoenig & Kenna, 1979). More recent data do not support this conclusion, and this author's clinical experience refutes the universality of these behaviors as necessary precursors of transsexualism.

In general, cross-dressers are motivated to wear and appear in female clothing to create the image of the female they perceive within themselves. The items of clothing are not erotically cathected; they are merely props that confirm an outer experience parallel to the inner experience of gender identity (Schaefer & Wheeler, 1995). But for the cross-dresser, although this desire to dress never disappears, it is not usually accompanied by a desire to alter the anatomy, revulsion toward the genitals, or a desire to live full-time in the female gender.

Additionally, the cross-dresser will report that a feeling of "tension" builds between periods of dressing and is only relieved by the act of cross-dressing.

Developmental psychologists who study primate behavior know that considerable time is spent in grooming and preening behaviors, which seem to occupy a high position in the hierarchy of behaviors, encoded in the brain. Perhaps the urge to cross-dress is similarly mandated by hormonally induced, critically timed modifications that occurred in utero. Or perhaps it is possible to conceptualize cross-dressing as behavior that provides dopamine-inducing rewards in the brain, promoting feelings that range from well-being to euphoria. Psychologist Richard Solomon (1980) has proposed a theoretical model, known as the opponent-process theory, that encompasses this possibility and explains a wide variety of acquired motivations.

According to this model, organisms behave in ways that keep bodily functions in a normative state: "The brains of all mammals are organized to oppose or suppress many types of emotional arousal or hedonic processes, whether they are pleasurable or aversive, whether they have been generated by positive or negative reinforcers." The opposing processes are automatically set in motion by events that induce disturbances in physiological or psychological systems. The disturbance, in turn, elicits counterreactions. After a given behavior occurs, resulting from the strong mammalian drive to "feel different" and inducing a rapid change in one's state, a cycle of "rush" and "craving" begins. This may be chemically mediated by the action of the neurotransmitter dopamine, which fires reward and euphoria circuits in the brain (Siegel, 1989).

Researcher George Rebec (1998) has provided collateral support for this model by studying how novel experiences affect dopamine in ways similar to stimulant drugs. To assess the precise way in which dopamine release occurs upon entry into a novel environment, Rebec uses a technology known as fast-scan cyclic voltammetry. This makes it possible to detect extremely small (nanomolar) amounts of dopamine in the extracellular fluid of the brain. Astonishingly, these measurements can be made every 100 milliseconds. This allows scientists, in the laboratory setting, to obtain real-time records of dopamine efflux from synaptic terminals, as animals engage in novel situations. Rebec concludes that, like recreational drugs, novelty promotes dopamine release. This effect seems to be restricted to a relatively small area of the limbic forebrain, known as the accumbal shell. This area receives input from many parts of the limbic system, which are thought to play a role in reinforcement. Thus, it appears that novelty and drugs of abuse share the same neurochemical system.

In 1996, Puri and Singh reported the case of a gender dysphoric patient who ceased cross-dressing when treated with 2 mg of pimozide daily. When, after one year, the dose was reduced to 1 mg, there was a rapid return of the cross-dressing behavior. An increase in the dose again led to a remission. Pimozide acts to block the reuptake of dopamine at neuronal receptors, allowing it to circulate in the synapses. Further studies on the role of dopaminergic agents on cross-dressing behavior may shed more light on this intriguing theory. For some cross-dressers, taking small doses of estrogenic compounds attenuates the desire to cross-dress, which at times may become unmanageable.

Typically, cross-dressers first experience the desire to wear clothing of the opposite sex just prior to, or contemporaneous with, puberty. Throughout adolescence and adulthood, the cross-dresser will purchase articles of clothing, or entire wardrobes, and hide them for fear of being discovered. Often this "binge" is followed by intense shame and an avowal to never cross-dress again. At this point, the cross-dresser "purges" and refrains from dressing for a period, possibly even for years. The desire to dress returns, and the cycle begins again. Some individuals have purchased and destroyed many wardrobes in the course of a lifetime.

Frequently, cross-dressers will limit themselves to wearing women's undergarments or stockings under typical male garb. Others will sleep in a female nightgown in the privacy of their own home to feel the comfort of being "oneself" if only for the duration of the night. Some fortunate individuals have family members or spouses who understand that cross-dressing feels natural and is essential to the well-being of the individual and thus are not bothered by the behavior. Many cross-dressers, however, store clothes in hidden locations and must look for rare, furtive opportunities to attain the fleeting harmony that cross-dressing affords.

Noting that the literature on cross-dressing men is generally limited to those who identified as patients at psychiatric clinics and were in distress, Brown et al. (1996) explored personality characteristics and sexual functioning in cross-dressers who had not sought treatment. These researchers found cross-dressers who were not seen for clinical reasons to be indistinguishable from non-cross-dressing men. They urged clinicians to utilize clinical significance criteria required by *DSM-IV* guidelines before diagnosing cross-dressers with an Axis I disorder.

Gender conditions are largely self-diagnosed. As we have seen, there is no test, chromosomal or psychological, that will render a medical diagnosis of gender dysphoria. Most clients come to therapists and disclose some measure of gender conflict, and then proceed from that point. Oftentimes, clients are clear and certain about their condition; others arrive confused and want more understanding of who they are and where they fit.

In some instances, individuals with issues other than gender dysphoria present, stating a desire for a "sex change." Individuals with thought disorders, such as schizophrenia, multiple personality disorder, Munchausen's syndrome, body dysmorphic disorder, transvestism with depression, or career female impersonators may be misdiagnosed as transsexual (Coleman, & Cesnik, 1990; Modestin & Ebner, 1995). While personality inventories such as the MMPI-2 cannot diagnose gender conflicts *per se,* they can be a valuable aid in elucidating psychopathology in cases where the gender condition appears to coexist with other psychiatric conditions. Therapists who are uncomfortable making a differential diagnosis to determine if a client has a gender identity condition or some other disorder should consult with a specialist in gender conditions. Likewise, therapists who suspect psychopathology in conjunction with gender issues should enlist the aid of a psychiatrist who is comfortable with gender-variant clients and can co-manage the case.

The following case is an example of a failure to consult with a specialist in gender conditions, when such consultation was sorely needed:

> The mother of a five-year old autistic boy brought the child to a clinic specializing in developmental and regulatory disorders of childhood. After a serious delay in language acquisition, the child began to verbalize that he is "a girl" and to dress in his sister's clothes. The child psychologist, who had never seen a case of gender identity disorder in childhood, told the mother that this was not really

a gender issue. She interpreted the behavior dynamically and reported that the child did not "feel safe as a boy." The mother left, confused as to how to proceed to resolve this, given the child's pervasive developmental delays. Both parents felt helpless and blamed themselves for not having provided a "safe" environment for their special needs child. In this case, the psychologist had practiced beyond the scope of her expertise. It behooved the clinician to find resources or referrals that address childhood gender disorders and provide serviceable and supportive options to the family.

Many persons who present with gender conditions will have some degree of attendant depression. Often the severity or intractable nature of the depression will require psychiatric consultation and pharmacological management. Consulting with a physician who understands the nature of gender conflicts will ease the anxiety of the patient, if he needs to be referred to another caregiver.

While the transsexual, like the cross-dresser, generally gives a history of cross-dressing throughout his lifetime, typically the feelings of the transsexual's cross-gender identification began in early childhood, rather than at puberty. As the *DSM-IV* criteria specify, there exists in these individuals a persistent and unremitting discomfort with the anatomic sex. The transsexual reports "living a lie" and feeling as though he or she has been born into the wrong body. This feeling is generally unwavering (previous *DSM* criteria specified continuous for two years). For some older individuals, there was a lack of awareness as adolescents or young adults that vehicles for changing their anatomy and gender existed. Once again, prior to knowledge of Christine Jorgensen, many individuals simply reconciled themselves to lives of desperation. Most often these clients now seek professionals to assist them with procuring hormones and/or surgeries so they can make the desired alterations of secondary sex characteristics and genitals.

Gender-variant clients generally range from 13 to 65 years, and this author has treated an 85-year-old male-to-female transsexual. Often, parents or grandparents present with concerns about children who are gender-variant. Some patients come to their first session dressed to express their preferred gender. Often clients arrive with a confused or angry spouse in tow.

Assessment of the client begins with thorough history-taking and interview to understand the client's self-perception and unique life map. This is an ongoing process that incorporates not only the obvious sex and gender inquiries, but also many other aspects of the client's life, including family issues, abuse issues, health particulars, previous psychotherapeutic endeavors, as well as social and occupational information. In constructing a representation of the client's world, it is important to understand not only his overt experiences, goals, and expectations, but also the nature of his fantasy life. This information is all grist for the therapeutic mill in making a differential diagnosis, and in assisting the client towards defining, refining, and meeting personal goals.

Diagnostically differentiating between the cross-dresser with acute gender dysphoria and the transsexual is often difficult. As we have seen, the previous division of cross-dressers into two categories—transsexuals and transvestites—based on whether there is accompanying fetishistic behavior, is overly simplistic and therapeutically unproductive. Brown (1990a) has suggested several lines of inquiry that may be serviceable in differentiating transsexualism from an intensification of gender dysphoria in a cross-dressing individual:

1. *What would happen if you stopped cross-dressing?* Transsexuals may be able to forgo cross-dressing for an extended period of time, if necessary, without experiencing the growing tension and anxiety described by the cross-dresser.

2. *Have you suffered any significant losses in the past two years?* Episodes of gender dysphoria in cross-dressing individuals often surface with intensity after the loss of a spouse, job, or other significant loss. The gender dysphoria of the transsexual is not loss-related, although the intensity of the dysphoria may also fluctuate over a lifetime.

3. *Do you sit or stand during urination? Do you touch your penis during urination and masturbation?* Cross-dressers and transvestites derive pleasure from their genitals and are not repulsed by them, in the way that transsexuals tend to be. Generally, transsexuals sit when urinating, and if they masturbate, they do so in a way that avoids direct genital contact.

Docter and Fleming (1992) developed a 55-item questionnaire to assess cross-genderism in adult males (see Appendix C). The subjects were 518 self-described heterosexual transvestites, 78 marginal transvestites ("borderline transsexuals"), and 86 transsexuals living full-time as women. Using factor analysis, four independent yet correlated factors emerge: cross-gender identity, cross-gender feminization, cross-gender social/sexual role, and cross-gender sexual arousal. With this instrument, gender nonconformity, both cognitive and behavioral, can be more precisely defined and operationalized.

Despite the inherent diagnostic value of such an instrument, Richard Docter warns that clinicians who work too hard at arriving at a "diagnosis" may be doing a disservice to their clients. An overzealous application of the medical model and its reliance on diagnosis (including self-diagnosis) may lead to rigid trajectories, generic treatment protocols, exaggeration or lying on the part of the patient, and grievous errors. Indeed, even among the group of individuals who are primary transsexuals, individual differences are great. Docter proposes that clinicians and clients use lines of inquiry suggested by the questionnaire to explore areas of behavior, cognition, and fantasy, and to assess their emotional valence to the client. Then, clinician and client can consider these factors and their implications for life choices (personal communication, August 25, 1998).

While research benefits from operational definition of theoretical constructs and the formulation of data-based typologies, clinical practice suffers from immoderate assumption of this ill-fitting model. Psychoeducational models that emphasize choice, uniqueness of individuals, and informed decision-making serve to depathologize gender variance while empowering individuals.

Female-to-Male Issues

Female-to-male clients present far fewer diagnostic uncertainties than male-to-female ones. First and foremost, all female-to-male transsexuals "cross-dress," but this behavior is not clinically remarkable as it does not violate social prohibitions. Neither is it fetishistic: Male items of clothing possess no erotic properties. Secondly, female-to-male transsexual persons often object to the term "transgendered," which implies a periodicity or fluidity of the phenomenon, which they do not feel accurately describes the immutable nature of their experience.

By the time the adult female-to-male approaches the health care system, he generally has a well-consolidated male identity. Futterweit (1998) has described the lack of ambivalence in this population thusly: "After following 92 such patients over the past 22 years, I have been impressed with several fascinating features of such patients. After adequate screening and psychiatric clearance, not one patient in this group has failed to go on to SRS. The compulsive, aggressive, and insatiable desire to become masculinized is inherent in all the f-t-m patients I have seen. Three patients who were 15 and 16 years of age (the latter were twins) had to be rejected temporarily until the age of

18 despite obvious criteria and characteristics of f-t-m trans-sexuals. Parenthetically, a number of these patients actually look quite masculine prior to treatment and engage in occupations and work frequently assigned to males (police officers, bartenders, heavy-duty laborers, etc.)."

Perhaps the greatest barrier to accurate diagnosis of the female-to-male transsexual is a lack of experience and knowledge on the part of the professionals whom they encounter, as the following example illustrates:

> Joshua is a twenty-year-old natal female who has been treated by fifteen psychiatrists, psychologists, and social workers in the past seven years. As a young child, Joshua [then Janet], was quite tomboyish, a phase the parents were convinced would pass, in time. When puberty arrived, the adolescent became markedly depressed and was taken to a psychiatrist. Janet reported to the doctor that she believed she should have been born a boy and wanted to live as a boy. The psychiatrist suggested to the parents that they tease the child about this if ever she mentioned such desires, or otherwise "make light" of any such utterances. This refusal on the part of the parents to "hear" any of Janet's dysphoric feelings, and the derision with which any cross-gender behavioral expressions were met, caused Janet to become withdrawn and remote. Although Janet was subjected to a number of different pharmaceutical and behavioral treatments by a sequence of mental health professionals, her sense of herself as a man never wavered.
>
> Finally, Janet contacted a social worker who had worked with several male-to-female transsexuals. Janet thought that this person could confirm her self-diagnosis and provide genuine assistance. But the social worked dismissed the possibility that she was a transsexual, based on her unwavering certainty that when she looked at Janet, "I can only see a girl." She was convinced that Joshua/Janet was a lesbian, although was admittedly unable to account for the client's avowed attraction to men.

Fortunately, Joshua's mother had attained a nursing degree in the years that her child was struggling with gender dysphoria, and she finally sought out a clinician who specialized in gender conditions. After interviewing both the mother and the client, the clinician was able to assist Joshua in finally beginning, in earnest, appropriate steps towards affirming his maleness.

It is interesting to note that Joshua was quite masculine appearing prior to any treatment, to the extent permitted by morphological parameters. The social worker who had counseled him was unable to entertain the notion that a masculine-looking person with large breasts could "be" anything other than the "girl" she "saw."

A 1979 study compared behavioral patterns in childhood and adolescence in female-to-male transsexuals and a matched group of lesbians. Both groups had a mean age of 21 years, 10 months. They did not differ in respect to the frequency of tomboy behavior, but the female-to-male group recalled preferring male peers more often. The groups differed significantly in regard to childhood cross-dressing: 80% of the transsexuals cross-dressed, as compared to 0% of the lesbians. The lesbians in this study reported no gender identity confusion in adolescence, and only 10% reacted negatively to breast development and onset of menses, in contrast to 70% of the female-to-male transsexuals (Ehrhardt, Grisanti, & McCauley).

Holly Devor (1993) uses the term *gender role relational style* to refer roughly to what others commonly call femininity and masculinity. According to Devor, "I use this term to emphasize that gender props are not the most important aspect of communicating gender to others; rather, styles of relating to others are among the strongest markers of gender." In the case of the female-to-male transsexual, the gender role relational style is unequivocally male. With hormonal assistance and chest surgery, the visible, telltale residue of femaleness recedes and successful identity consolidation can proceed.

7

Gender Variance and the Formation of the Self

I have no problem doing what I need to do to make myself comfortable in the world. . . if only everyone I know would wake up tomorrow morning with amnesia. — A transsexual on gender transition

Those who work with transgendered clients, or merely read the autobiographies of transsexuals, are struck by the similarities of their historical self-reflections. There is, first, the burgeoning awareness on the part of the child that the self is not compatible with the body, that one is not what one appears outwardly to be. Subsequently, there follows the inevitable pain upon learning that the real self must be concealed, for it is fundamentally unacceptable.

This process occurs in childhood, long before the child cognitively understands that gender problems are social problems. It occurs before the child is able to grasp that gender problems are tragically misunderstood, threatening to a parental sense of competence, and mistakenly linked to issues of sexuality. The child who innocently expresses the wish or the belief that he or she is of, or will change into, the desired gender, is met with disapproval, if not outright punishment.

One male-to-female transsexual recalls spending days as a youngster building a beautiful, well-designed, and elaborate doll house. When the father saw this masterful creation, he remarked, "Boys don't build doll houses." This person, now an adult, can still recall, with painful affect, the shame of that moment. Truly, shame is the primary method by which gender roles are inculcated.

Psychoanalysis, which began as a conceptual system to understand psychopathological behavior, developed later into a method of treatment, and finally evolved into a theory of personality (Corsini, 1977). As we know, this theory holds that the mind is a battleground and various forces clashing—struggles between the conscious and the unconscious—create emotional disturbances. According to Freud, the libidinal attitudes that children necessarily develop toward the parents, along with the attempts to resolve the anxiety engendered by this situation, are the antecedents to many neuroses and psychoses, including transsexual "wishes."

The neo-Freudians broke with Freud's deterministic view of personality. These psychoanalytic deviationists, Adler, Fromm, and Horney, added important elements to personality theory, including the concepts of cognition, values, and goals, thereby constructing a more comprehensive understanding of the human psyche. But it was the psychiatrist Harry Stack Sullivan who in 1953, with the publication of *The Interpersonal Theory of Psychiatry,* made an enormous contribution, with particular import for the study of gender conditions. Sullivan was the first to theorize that relationships with other people help form personality. This social-psychiatric perspective was a radical departure from previous views. Moreover, Sullivan, like Erik Erikson, was a developmentalist. He traced the formation of personality, from infancy to adulthood, and outlined the social challenge that must be mastered at each and every stage for successful, healthy integration of personality to occur.

Sullivan recognized that there are two realities: inner and outer. The self-system develops only in relation to others, as the experience of the "me" distinguishes itself from the "not-me" based on the reflected appraisals from others. One particular phase of development has unparalleled significance for the healthy emergence of self. It is the preadolescent epoch.

Sullivan recognized that the need for playmates like oneself, a need for interpersonal intimacy, first begins in preadolescence, somewhere between eight and a half and ten years of age. This interest in a close friend, or chum, is crucial to the formation of identity and implies the development of empathy that is akin to love. This love of the friend has nothing to do with genital contact, but is a closeness that permits "validation of all components of personal worth." Sullivan believed that through positive observation of the self in interaction with the chum there existed inherent psychotherapeutic possibilities:

> During the juvenile era a number of influences of vicious family life may be attenuated or corrected. . . . Because one draws so close to another, because one is newly capable of seeing oneself through the other's eyes, the preadolescent phase of personality development is especially significant in correcting autistic, fantastic ideas about oneself or others. I would like to stress—at the risk of using superlatives which sometimes get very tedious—that development of this phase of personality is of incredible importance. . . . I would hope that preadolescent relationships were intense enough for each of the two chums literally to get to know practically everything about the other one that could be exposed in an intimate relationship, because that remedies a good deal of the often illusory, usually morbid, feeling of being different, which is such a striking part of . . . insecurity in later life. (pp. 247-8, 256)

For the preadolescent with gender conflicts, there is no possibility of this intense intimacy, for the authentic self cannot be disclosed. The child, instead of attaining the longed-for validation, develops what Sullivan called a "pseudoself," a personification that protects against social ostracism. The interactions with peers cannot be intense and are often avoided altogether, for fear that the concealed self might inadvertently bleed through. It is during this time that the experience of loneliness first arises—an experience Sullivan describes as "so terrible that it baffles clear recall, more terrible than anxiety." It is this terrible loneliness that transsexuals often bring to the therapeutic encounter, a loneliness that does not end in adulthood.

The pseudoself functions like a "shell" that belies the very existence of an inner, real self. The fundamental plight of the transsexual is that the world—what Sullivan termed "significant others"—relates to the person as though he or she were the shell. This creates a continuous internal ecology of always feeling misunderstood and having to behave uncharacteristically, in order to meet society's expectations.

The following material introduces a male-to-female transsexual patient named Kristen. Here, in her own words, she describes the feelings that result from the incongruity of her inner and outer selves. The anguish, the ultimate acceptance, and the determination to resolve her dilemma through gender transition are expressed in journal entries. Experienced therapists will recognize in this remarkable account every aspect of the challenges that face the transgendered individual, for all are encountered and described in this moving testimony. The decision to make this life change is one that she has to justify—not only to herself but to society as well.

Kristen's Journey

This is the story of a long journey to today, and hopefully, to far beyond.

December 1992

My ancient history has elements of many such stories: I suffered physical abuse over an extended period when young, had an emotionally distant father, became aware at the age of four of wanting to be a girl, experimented with my sister's clothes, felt joy then guilt, felt confusion as puberty came along and I was attracted to girls both because I loved them and because I wanted to be them, attempted suicide at sixteen, had intensive counseling to "cure" me of wanting to be a woman.

After college I married a "wonderful" woman who at first said my cross-dressing didn't matter and then had trouble dealing with it, was divorced after fifteen years of marriage (no children to complicate the issue), entered immediately into another relationship with a woman, probably believing that she could "save" me from my wanting to be a woman, then moved from the big city to a rural state when that relationship ended, quickly fell in love with another woman, hoping to live a "normal" life, to be saved, only to have that relationship fail when she realized she couldn't deal with the cross-dressing. I then had a one-month relationship with a woman who had been a good friend until then. Somehow that got screwed up.

Now we are up to early August. I am forty-five years old, have a decent job, a wonderful house in a picturesque location, but my subconscious is screaming "Now is the time; now go for what you want; become the woman you are."

But my conscious mind wouldn't listen. I can't sleep, I start to drink too much, and I start to think thoughts of suicide. However, my conscious mind doesn't know why I am feeling so depressed. Oh, sure, it knows that I want to be a woman, but it knows all the reasons why that can't happen.

My therapist tries to help me, and she asks me why I wouldn't go ahead with what I want. So I rehearse for her the reasons I have been using for years: I am too old (wouldn't we all wish to be young women if we could be—with years of experiences ahead of us?), I have a comfortable life that would be shattered if I went ahead with this. I would probably lose my job and my house, and the latter would really hurt, because for the first time, I feel I am "home." I have too much body hair and it would take years of electrolysis to have it removed, and on and on and on.

So summer stretches into fall, and my depression deepens to the point that every weekend I visit a different location in this rural state and decide how I will commit suicide. I even make a list of the places I find and the advantage and disadvantage of each.

But while all this is going on, my subconscious is fighting to be heard. In May, I located an illegal source of hormones, and I started taking them, believing in the evidence in the literature that very low dosages of hormones can deter potential transsexuals from becoming "full blown" transsexuals. And in July, I started to collect information from those T* (transvestite, transgendered, transsexual) bulletin boards about their hormone usage for an FAQ (frequently asked questions); and I spent nearly every lunch time in the library reading T* books and articles I had read years ago.

My conscious mind was denying the obvious purpose of all this, and my subconscious mind was doing all it could to be heard—and thus the two were like two trains steaming towards each other on the same track. I was a crisis waiting to happen.

Finally it did; in November I attempted suicide again, but, as we know, many suicides are simply calls for help, and thus are often done in such a way that they will not succeed. So in my case—I lived through my attempt—but my subconscious got its way, the suicide got the voice of the subconscious heard.

More intensive counseling, and then, in the middle of the night near Thanksgiving, I had the worst anxiety attack of my life. I thought my heart would explode; I was covered with sweat, but I couldn't figure out what I was so anxious about. Of course, it just so happened that I had counseling the next day, but in the middle of the night, I didn't put two and two together. (Of course, my subconscious mind had.)

At the session that day, my therapist and I talked about the anxiety attack, about my continuing thoughts of suicide, and she asked me again to list the reasons why I didn't want to go ahead and live as a woman. As I listed each reason, it was like the sun burst through the window: the whole room became lighter and I could "see" my future; each reason seemed silly in comparison to the happiness I now felt in consciously embracing the possibility of sex reassignment surgery (SRS). She could see in my face my decision, and simply said "It has been a long road, hasn't it?"

That night I called my sister and told her of my decision to become a woman. It was a great call; she challenged me to explain my needs and reasons and helped me to think through the issues even better. Over the next week, I told the rest of the female members of my family (found it hard to tell my brothers), I legally went on hormones and Spironolactone, started electrolysis, and told a dozen of my friends and co-workers. Several said they weren't surprised, none seemed to have a problem with it. (Thank goodness many of us in this state take a private approach to religion, so I have no fundamentalists to worry about.) Some of those people told their children, who, by and large, seem to have taken it better and accepted it more quickly.

The euphoria wore off, and I have begun to make plans for "transitioning," wondering how they will take it at work, but not particularly caring. I am going to take the hard road—do it here, in full view of society, à la Renee Richards, trying to keep my job and friends instead of moving to a new city and beginning there where people don't know me. Oh sure, I know the difficulties of this approach—at the very least 90% of the people I come into contact with at work shall know of my biological past—and working in a University as I do, the students shall pass that on to each new generation of students. Outside the University it is a small, rural world, and they will know—but it is also a community that leaves people alone.

Depression set in when I realized how little help there is for me in this part of America. There are no gender clinics, few other transsexuals, and so no one to turn to for advice, support, or a shoulder to lean on. There is no easy way to get advice on SRS, to hear stories of making the transition, etc.

I knew I would survive. After all, I have until now as a man; I just need to hold on a little longer until I can become the woman I guess I would have wished to marry—a strong, independent woman who does her job well, has a few close friends, and cares about them.

Winter 1993

In January I fell into a really deep depression; I missed suicide only because the logging truck that was coming towards me (I was in his lane) swerved at the last moment. I realized a few days later that I was so depressed because of a failure I was having in contacting pre- and post-op transsexuals to get advice and to talk about their experiences. In this rural state, there is no support available of any type, and I hoped that I would be able to get such via e-mail. Many post-ops failed to respond, and the advice from pre-ops greatly varied. Some said don't transition on the job—leave the city, state, etc.; others said stay on the job and don't run.

My depression resulted, I realized, because I was waiting for someone to give me a road map of how to get from X to the RLT (Real Life Test) and beyond. I wanted a text book. I pulled out of the depression when I realized there is no text book because there is no right and wrong here. Each of us comes to this point from many different places and with different baggage. And each of us has to walk the road that is correct for her. February went well; I slowly started to tell trusted friends.

And I suppose the inevitable happened—I received some strong challenges to my plans (all well-meaning of course). Two examples follow:

> *Dear Dr. Rachael,*
> *As a biologically-determined female living within my*

female gender I have developed a feminist outlook because of the way society views women. I would like to know how you, as a biologically-determined male proposing to live within a female gender, will feel. I find it frustrating knowing that women are second-class citizens, socially, economically even spiritually. We receive less for our efforts, fewer rewards for them, and little credit for our inner strengths (which aren't always "feminine ones"). Many women suffer. A few succeed. Most of us cope.

In this world where so much blame, hatred and mistrust is meted out to women, how can you, born a man with all the "advantages" society gives you, be so willing to give all that up to live as a woman? I perceive in you, in what I have heard second or third hand, a strong desire for the accouterments of a feminine ideal—the clothes, the hair, the very feminine name—but I really want to know if you are willing to understand and put up with all that it takes to be a female in a man's world.

I responded in part:

You ask if I am "willing to understand and put up with what it takes to be a female in a man's world." This is a very fair question, but I think you will agree that I can answer that question honestly only when I have, indeed, lived as a woman for some period of time. Otherwise I would simply be paying lip service to my supposedly liberal nature. Oh, it is true that, over the years, I have witnessed much of what you describe regarding the way in which society treats, or more appropriately, mistreats women.

However, I cannot pretend that I will ever truly know the full degree of the "blame, hatred and mistrust . . .

*meted out to women." Certainly, I shall experience some
of that, but most of the negative reaction I shall receive
will come from the fact that nearly all around me know
that I am neither male nor female but transsexual. At the
worst, in the minds of some, I will be seen as a freak of
nature and something to be despised. In the minds of
others, I shall be viewed as a threat or challenge to their
own conceptions of gender and behavior.*

*You also ask "how I can be so willing to give up (all
the advantages society gives men) to live as a woman?"
Again, a very fair question and I will have to admit that
I am cheating in this respect. I am not, like many other
transsexuals, abandoning my current life, my friends, my
job, and my home to start over in a city where no one
knows of me, taking on a job and salary that society
may choose for me because I am perceived to be female.
On July 6, I will bring with me into my new life the
achievements that I have accrued in 46 years as a male.*

*If I had been born a woman, I am certain that would
have stood in the way of some of my achievements. For
example, I can well imagine that such attitudes would
have made it difficult for me to earn a Ph.D. from the
University of Chicago in only three years while being
married (as I was); they would have made it difficult for
me to hold the succession of jobs that I have; they would
have made it difficult for me to be chosen for this job.*

*But, of course, the true question is not where I have
come from as a man, but where I shall go from here.
And the irony is that I fully realize my career progression
is probably over. Were I a genetic woman and had the
achievements above, I undoubtedly could go on to a
much better job from here; as a transsexual, however, I
shall be able to go no further up the ladder. I shall be a
victim of the "blame, hatred and mistrust meted out to*

transsexuals." So how shall I do in this new life? From extensive communication with others, I know that many who have made this journey before me have suffered, a few have chosen to end their life, some have coped, and very, very few have succeeded. But this is the row I have chosen to hoe.

Finally, in some minds there may be a question as to whether in the future I shall presume to make judgments about the experiences of women and whether I shall presume to speak for them as if I did, indeed, understand the full nature of their suffering. To do so would be an act of extreme hubris. No, the life I shall live will be that of a sexual bastard, the illegitimate offspring of the male and female genders, metaphorically carrying something of each gender without having the right to claim my place in either.

But I shall survive.

Why am I "so willing to give up all the 'advantages' that society gives men . . . to live as a transsexual?"

I don't know; I simply know I must.

Following is my response to a more spirited challenge from another:

Dear X,

I read your letter, it appears a major concern of yours is whether, by choosing this course of action, I am to miss out on certain experiences/opportunities that I could only have as a male. Yes, certainly, that is true. But does that matter? To live is to make choices, and each of these choices opens as many doors as it closes. Over a decade ago, I had a vasectomy. Would you have written me the same letter suggesting I not have a vasectomy because I would never know the joy of being a parent? And would you have argued, as in essence later in your letter, that having a vasectomy would be to argue with "God" since I denied a possibility (having a child) that "God" gave me?

You ask, quoting the EST training, "Can you afford the arrogance that no such thing exists, the knowing of which, your life would be transformed?" And later you write, "Our gender is like a little block of granite that God assigns to us, it is where we place our feet in the Universe, and it is hubris, the most frightful hubris, to argue with God on this matter." I would like to address these together, because I believe they are the same question.

You ask whether I have the arrogance, the hubris, to question the hand dealt to me by life—whether I have the arrogance, the hubris, to refuse to accept the decision of God in the gender assigned to me. I believe you know I do not believe in a God which directs or even cares about the lives of individuals, but accepting your appeal to God as a metaphor for the natural biological patterns into which we find ourselves of humankind, and the lessons of much of the Bible tell us that our lives are a trial and that we must, in our own ways, confront the burdens placed before us. The trials of Job, of Sarah, the lesson from the Last Supper, in fact, the entire life of Jesus, would have us believe that humankind must, in the face of great odds and social approbation, find and follow the right path. It is too easy to suggest that we should play the hand dealt to us. May I suggest that too often we have not looked at our cards carefully enough? I have; I have found a wild card in the hand; and I intend to play it.

I recall that in a separate conversation you suggested that God placed each of us on this earth for a reason;

although I cannot subscribe to that belief, I simply wish to counter that, in the context perhaps my reason for being here is to have the operation, to change my life in this manner, so I can demonstrate to others that if I can take such an action, then they can take smaller actions which their fear or society has, until now, prevented them from taking. But I cannot argue this line too long; it runs against my grain. My actions are mine, and yours are yours, and their interactions are random and undirected. The excitement comes from working through those interactions. . . . Finally, you ask if there is a possibility that I have mistaken my attraction to women for wanting to be one. Perhaps my desire does flow from my lifelong love of women, but this cause and effect concern you raise here (and elsewhere) is not of interest to me. Would it matter if you knew why your son has little interest at present to certain things you hold dear? The cause is unimportant, the effect is the element you wish to comprehend and perhaps modify.

I began plans for July and I drafted a letter to send to some 250 administrators here at the University. I planned on transitioning in July, and I planned to release the letter two months before that.

In early March, however, I started to get feedback that there was a rumor going around campus that I was going to do this—however, the rumor was low-key and isolated to certain parts. In mid-March, I got a call from a trusted friend that the rumor was everywhere and was spreading off campus. The next day, I met with my boss, my senior staff, and the following day I had a group meeting with my twenty clerical staff. I told each of my decision, handed them a copy of the yet-to-be-issued letter explaining everything, and allowed plenty of time for reaction. At the clerical meeting, I had a Ph.D. clinical psychologist with me.

The letter was then sent to the administrators:

March 19, 1993

To: The President, Vice president, Deans, Assistant Deans, Chairs, and Directors

From: Peter Rachael, Director of Business Services

There is no good way to begin this letter except to say that on July 6, I will begin living as a woman. My name will be legally Kristen, and to all intents and purposes, on that date, Peter will no longer legally exist.

I suffer from a condition called gender dysphoria. Simply put, my gender does not align with my genetic sex. This is not an acquired condition; rather, it is an intrinsic part, a lifelong aspect of my being. It is a rare condition, to be sure, but one extensively studied and with a generally accepted medical treatment.

There is no easy way to explain to you the basis for this condition or decision, nor can I expect that you will completely understand the full nature of how I feel. In fact, medical and mental health professionals with extensive education, training, and experience in this area do not truly know how their patients feel.

The influences which cause a person to develop this conflict between their gender and their biologically deter mined sex can be described as pre- or post-natal (pre- or post-birth). Current research indicates that the most like ly pre-natal cause for gender dysphoria can be found in certain hormonal imbalances at a critical point in the development of the fetus. The result is that an individual can develop having the anatomical features of one sex while having the gender of the other.

Post-natal influences on gender dysphoria are typically believed to come from family structure and attitudes and certain societal responses to gender typing. However, it is simply not possible to say that a certain type of childhood experience will result in gender dysphoria. In fact, studies show that gender dysphoric individuals, in general, have a childhood that is more similar to that experienced by most other children than it is dissimilar (both in its positive and negative experiences).

Over time, various solutions have been suggested by the medical and mental health communities to resolve this conflict, but the only one that has been found to be effective to date is for the individual to live as their gender rather than as their biological sex.

I became aware of my female gender identity at about the age of four. I have spent a good part of my life struggling with this conflict between my body and my mind. I have studied this subject in depth, I have been treated by professionals, but I have also spent a great deal of time and effort hiding, denying and trying, to no avail, to be "normal," to purge my female gender identity.

Finally I gradually came to accept that my gender dysphoria is part of who I am as a person; it is part of the reality of my being. I have slowly followed a course of action to find peace and harmony and comfort with my gender. On July 6, my biological birthday, I will effect the physical birthday of the gender I wish to have for the rest of my life. Since making the decision, I have found an inner peace that I have never felt before, but I know that the foreseeable future will be a time of great stress for me. And I know there will be stress for some of you.

Sex is a rigid barrier for most of us, and to see someone crossing that boundary is disconcerting. I have no desire to cause feelings of discomfort in anyone, but I hope some of you will find a way to tolerate my decision even if you cannot endorse it. I have chosen to make the announcement of my plans in this public manner, and at this time, so as to allow people to work through the implications of what I am doing, and, if they wish, to discuss the matter with me well before the transition date I have chosen. This has not been an easy letter to write, and it probably has not been an easy letter for you to read. Over the past few months, I have told a small number of friends of my decision, and in doing so, I have learned that people need time to work through the implications of what I have told them, to place my decision in their own terms. I have also learned that people typically have many questions to ask.

The success of my transition will depend on my being open and honest with everyone, and this is the reason for this letter. I am more than willing to answer any and all questions you might have, and I invite you, if you wish, to call me or to discuss the matter with me in person. There are no "dumb" questions as they relate to gender dysphoria; I had to research this for years, and I still do not understand all of it.

I want to conclude by thanking those of you who welcomed Peter several years ago when I returned to my native state from "away," and I hope you will be able to accept Kristen in the future.

I waited for the explosion: none came.

Rather, I started to get calls of support and notes of support. The President and each Vice President wrote, as did people I didn't know.

But this was four months before I planned to transition. Too much time for people to get worked up. Two weeks after the memo went out, I got a call from the local newspaper (only two in the state), saying that they were going to do a story on me, quoting from my memo. I fought it, quoting anonymity, but they felt I was a public figure. I finally agreed to an interview to hope to put a human face on the "freak" article, but then wrote the following to the editor:

Ms. Joan Smith
Editor, Style Section
Daily News

Dear Ms. Smith:

As you know, I reluctantly agreed to be interviewed by Tom Weber about my planned gender change when I learned that The Daily News *intended to do a story with or without my "permission." By allowing an interview, I hoped to minimize the likelihood of a negative article. However, as I explained to you, I felt, and still do, that the matter of my gender change is not an appropriate subject to appear in a newspaper.*

At the least, the article is an invasion of my privacy; at the worst, its publication smacks of sensationalism.

On the issue of privacy, it is true that I notified many members of the University community of my plans, but unlike your readership, members of the University must work with me each day and they need to decide how my change will affect them. This is not the case with your readership; very few who were ignorant of my plans before your article will have to deal with me: absolutely none need to know of my change.

On the issue of sensationalism, I ask whether you would have run the article if I had worked for a private firm instead of the University, or if my problem had been, instead, AIDS, cancer, or mental illness. Likewise, I wonder why you did not consent to running the article without using my name or work affiliation.

Certainly, this article has made a private matter intensely public; I will have to suffer the consequences of

*your decision to publish the article. And sadly, so will
that portion of your readership which suffers from sexual identity questions or other problems since each will
fear that his or her private life, like mine, could become
fodder for the* Daily News.

Peter Rachael

March 31, 1993

The letter apparently worked—although she did not agree to
kill the article, she agreed to run it anonymously. Except, they
forgot to delete one reference to the University—and they ran
an enormous picture of me.

It was in their weekend edition, which is distributed throughout the state, and the article was next to Dave Barry's column.
Rather appropriate, I thought.

Reprinted without permission, but who cares—they were
going to quote from my memo without my permission.

A Search For Gender Identity

After a lifetime of feeling he was a woman trapped in a
man's body, a sex change was the answer he chose
(*Editor's note*—At the interviewee's request, names
have been changed.)

By Tom Weber, News Senior Writer

After more than 40 years or unhappiness and confusion,
of feeling so at odds with himself and the world that suicide seemed to be the only solution, Scot decided to radi-
cally alter his life.

He explained his decision on March 19 in a letter to 250
employees of the large institution where he has worked for
two years. Having wrestled for weeks with the proper
wording, he chose an opening paragraph guaranteed to
raise more than a few eyebrows and questions:

"There is no good way to begin this letter except to say

that on July 6, I will be living my life as a woman. My name will be legally Kristen Rachael, and to all intents and purposes, on that date, Scot will no longer legally exist."

With the letter in circulation, he waited for the storm of protest that he supposed would follow so startling an announcement. Yet instead of losing his high-ranking position, a possibility he anticipated, he received a letter of support from his boss.

Claiming that as long as Scot's performance and health remained satisfactory, and the performance of those who worked with him was not adversely affected, his boss and he looked forward to working with Scot, regardless of his gender.

While some of Scot's friends and colleagues found his decision to be morally troubling and even bizarre, their responses so far have been more compassionate than hostile.

"I care what happens to Scot. He's a human being and a kind person," said Donna, who works for Scot. "But it's hard to believe this is going to make him happy. I'm afraid what my reaction will be when he walks into the office with a dress on. This state, or at least this part of the state, may not be ready for this."

Scot, who said he expected anger and frustration, is delighted about the support and understanding he has received.

"I'm pleased to say that I've had some very good responses, even a nice letter," he said recently at his office. "I have yet to get a negative letter, but I expect it. Sex is a rigid barrier for most of us, and to see someone crossing that boundary is disconcerting."

"Many people thought I was a homosexual—I'm not. When those people saw me dating women, they knew it was more complex. But the sexual part is not the issue here. It's the last thing on my mind. I'm not doing this to have sex with men, but to live the life I've always wanted."

Born in Portland in 1947, the oldest of four children, Scot said he sensed at the age of four that something was wrong with him.

"Even then I was conscious of being uncomfortable

with my body," said Scot, who wore a white shirt, tie, dress slacks, a touch of mascara and flounce elastic securing his ponytail. "I had dreams of being a girl, and enjoyed playing more with my younger sister than with the boys in the neighborhood. I thought that if I just believed, I would grow up to be a girl, it would happen. Of course it didn't."

His largely unhappy childhood evolved into pubescent crisis. Not only was he attracted to girls, he wanted to be one—to incorporate in himself those very female qualities he found so desirable. At a private all-male school in Massachusetts, Scot attempted suicide for the first time. He was kicked out. After intensive psychotherapy, during which he was introduced to his baffling condition known as "gender dysphoria," he returned to the school and graduated with high honors.

"Therapy taught me coping mechanisms, though I was never reconciled to my gender," he said.

Scot got a bachelor's degree in 1969 from the University of Chicago. Two years later, after having dated "a string of girlfriends" in college, he got married. Scot said that 60 percent of transsexuals such as himself do, in fact, have heterosexual relationships. While Scot's wife knew he liked to dress in women's clothing, she asked only that he not do it in her presence.

"I was married for 15 years," he said. "there was a strain on the marriage, sure, but it wasn't an issue of great concern. The marriage broke up not because of the gender dysphoria, but because we were both professionals and moved our separate ways. We had no children."

After receiving a doctorate in educational administration, Scot forged a successful career at the University of Chicago. Two years ago, tired of the city life that caused him to become cold and uncaring, he moved back here to take his present job.

A year ago, still desperately struggling with his "gender identity," tried to kill himself for the second time. After surviving yet another suicide attempt last November, Scot said he knew he could not continue living in denial. He would finally have to undergo the sex-change operation that would join his warring physical and emotional selves.

"I came to the critical point and decided there would never be a good time to do it, that now was a good time." he said. "I reviewed all the possibilities—that I could lose my job, my friends, my home. But I had no choice. This couldn't be counseled out of me."

Before going public with his letter, Scot assembled his clerical staff to gauge their reaction to his plan. The employees were from small rural towns, many with families whose roots in this area ran deep. One woman asked Scot why he decided to undergo his dramatic transformation here, and not in a more anonymous setting like Boston or New York.

"I asked her what her reaction would be if her husband said he was being transferred to Connecticut, and that she would be cut off from all she knew," Scot said. "It's the same for me. When I came here two years ago, I had friends, a house. I've put down roots here, too, and I'm loathe to pull them up. Now, for the first time in my life, I feel like a whole person."

On the morning of July 6, his 46th birthday, Scot will choose a female business outfit from his closet, do his hair and makeup and walk into the office as a woman named Kristen. He has already begun the electrolysis that he hopes will have smoothed his face by then. The female hormones he has been taking since November will eventually soften the angularity of his slender body.

He said he will feel terribly self-conscious when greeting his employees at first, just as they will feel uncomfortable greeting their boss.

"It will bother me," Donna said. "I just can't imagine him as a woman. I will respect him, as I do now, but I really think he's going to make himself more of an outcast than he feels he is already."

Elliot, a data-processing coordinator who works next door to Scot, said his religious beliefs will never allow him to accept his boss's decision. Yet Elliot said he, too, will continue to respect Scot for his skills and professionalism he has always brought to the work place

"I'm a Jehovah's Witness, so in a personal way I feel this goes against what is natural," Elliot said. "But will it impact what I do here? No, I have developed a lot of respect for what he's done here. We're good business partners. So whether he is in a male's outfit or a female's doesn't make a difference to me. I don't think this has a negative effect on the University."

If, after a year of living as a woman, he is still determined to take the next crucial step, Scot will go to either Colorado, Wisconsin, or Canada to undergo the surgery that will give him—within anatomical limits—a woman's body. After that, he said, the process he should have begun years ago will have been completed.

"Would I have wished for a different life if I could do it over again? Well, this has been a part of me for so long, I couldn't imagine it not being this way," he said. "If I could have pushed a button 20 years ago and lived a normal life, and not have gone through the grief, I would have. On the other hand, I wouldn't push that button now. Finally, I am able to change my gender and damn it, I'm going to do it."

In early April, three months to the Real Life Test (RLT), the period of living as a woman, the real grief begins. Several members of my clerical staff are agitating against me (Why are you putting us through this; why do we have to quit our jobs if we can't take your appearance after July 6; why doesn't the University make you leave?). And then, Donna, the woman quoted twice in the article, and an employee of mine, decides to fall in love with me—and doesn't want me to go ahead with my plans.

July 1993

Real ups and downs all spring. Donna is making my life both great and miserable, the staff continues to agitate, I get tired of the time I have to wait, especially as I read on Transgen of people who decide one day and transition two weeks later.

When I believed I was a transvestite (TV), I never saw in the mirror anything but "a guy in makeup." But, and here is the strange thing, after I made the decision in November to go for the RLT, I did not get completely dressed up once. At the time, I rationalized it away by saying that I was going to hold off until the big day. In fact, I think I was worried that I would continue to see just "a guy in makeup" and I would chicken out of the RLT.

In making the decision for the RLT, I had told myself that, no matter what I looked like on July 6, that was the life I was going to lead. After all, I had made the decision because I could no longer live as Peter. He wasn't then, and never really had been the whole me.

So, it was an absolutely incredible thing when, on the first day of the RLT, I dressed up, put on my makeup, did my hair and faced the world.

For the first time, this was real, and because of this it did not matter to me that I wasn't good looking. (Don't we sometimes use as an excuse for not transitioning that we will never be as good looking as we wish we could be.) However, on that first day, looking back at me was the face and body of an average woman, and I smiled.

But, a step back.

By the beginning of July, I had gone through 180 hours of electrolysis, six hours of private makeup lessons, and, of course, countless hours of psychotherapy. (As someone advised me early on, get your act together before your change, because after the change it is sometimes hard to separate change issues from nonchange issues.)

I had also purchased more clothes than my savings account could safely cover. Early on, I had decided that, after years of wearing men's clothes, I would never wear women's business suits. So, after twenty-five years of admiring the taste of career women in Chicago, I found my taste running to upscale "career" dressing.

July 6 actually arrived as these things have a tendency to do. After taking the 40 minute drive from my home to campus and parking my car in the lot, I checked myself out in the mirror, adjusted my handbag, grabbed my bottled water and walked into work. I had already decided that I would not alter my daily routine, and so, as I do every morning, I said hello to each of my employees, and then I went about my day as if I had always been Kristen. As usual, I went to the student union for lunch, and I took a walk across the campus in the mid-afternoon. In short, I acted as if the day were a normal one, and I hoped people would act the same. As several had suggested, I always acted confidently and did not make as much eye contact with others as some men are apt to do.

And things went incredibly well. Even the employee who I knew was having the biggest problem with my change came into my office soon after I arrived and she wished me well. Other staff members clearly found the change jolting, but they continued to treat me in a professional way. However, something started to surprise me: those who knew me and knew of my change looked at me and even commented, but the many who didn't know me acted as if nothing were wrong—that is, they seemed to believe that I was, indeed a woman. I naturally assumed they were being polite, because I just knew that I must have a big sign on my front and back saying "man in a dress, look away!"

So, later in the week, I did the real test and went to Wal-Mart and to a busy supermarket. I expected the gawkers and the whispering, but they never came. Oh sure, I did catch a few double takes, but after the second look, the expected gawking did not occur. Maybe the second look was just to satisfy the person that this six-foot, slender woman was, indeed, exactly what she appeared to be. So, either there was an incredible agreement amongst the entire population of my home town that they will act as if there is nothing unusual about a "man in a dress," or I must be presenting just enough of the necessary visual and body language signals, so that their subconscious minds accept those signals as female, and do not send the dreaded "check out that person" message to interrupt the conscious mind's weighty contemplation of when the heat will break, or how the Red Sox are doing.

When I stopped by my hairdresser to change my appointment, she didn't recognize me at first, and at a ribbon-cutting ceremony later in the week, two of my "fellow" administrators stood beside me for five minutes and seemingly reacted with honest surprise when I said hello.

Fall 1993

So now, it is months later, and the good and the bad continues. Several members of my staff continue to give me grief, Donna continues to try to make me pull back, and there is always the fear of being "read" in public, but I have come to grips with that.

I know that one of my greatest fears was the ridicule I believed I would face transitioning openly, in a rural state, in a job of relative visibility, in an academic setting.

I sometimes wonder if we fail to realize how wide is the range of female appearance. In agonizing over whether to change, I know that I filtered my perceptions through the cultural stereotype of the beautiful woman. It was when I realized that I could no longer be Peter that I no longer cared how I would end up looking.

Allison L., in one of her videotapes, said something that made me pause and rerun the segment. She said that she doesn't worry about passing; she simply wants to be accepted as a woman, i.e. the waitress, the town clerk, the person at the DMV, may know full well that we are not genetic women, but the important thing is that we are accepted and treated with due respect.

Certainly, passing is important, but acceptance is especially important for those of us who are doing our RLT in full view of those who knew us in our male personas. With these people, it is not an issue of passing; many will never see us without that little voice in their head saying, "that is really Peter." But while they may not be able to accept us as genetic women, if they no longer see us as male, then we have won much of the battle.

But we must also do things to help them accept us as women. A friend wrote to me telling me how difficult it was to get her colleagues to accept her as a woman. I suggested that she wear to work only dresses and skirts for three weeks—i.e., no slacks. She found it made a difference; they needed help in making the mental transition from her male persona to her female persona.

Oh, I am not saying that we cannot wear slacks, jeans, etc. Nor am I saying that we should dress as if we were going to the theater when we are just going out to breakfast. What I am simply saying is that, during the RLT, it became real, at least for me, because I was fostering an environment in which people, and I myself, could see me as a woman and not simply as "a guy in makeup." We need to give them enough gender signals so their subconscious minds can read us as women, or if we do not spend that much time with our image, at least not register anything that will cause the second look.

But as I noted, acceptance is also critical. I spent a Sunday afternoon recently in a bar in a fishing village, the bar filled with rowdy fishermen who, because of the gale winds, had been unable to venture out into the cold Atlantic. Some "read" me or perhaps wondered. The majority didn't, but no one seemed to care. No snickering, no sideways glances. (Oh, no, I don't usually hang out in such locations, they happen to make great fish chowder, and that was just what I wanted on a damp, wind-driven gray Sunday.)

January 1994

I now have a date for surgery: May 26 in Neenah, Wisconsin, with Dr. Eugene Schrang, perhaps the best SRS surgeon in the

U.S. Too many people view the surgery as the primary event; with the proper attitude, the surgery is just a rest stop on the journey. If the goal is to change gender, to be who we have wished and needed to be for years, then the RLT is the big event. To the public we are women upon beginning the RLT. Most do not know we have not had the surgery; those who do know quickly forget and then are surprised when they hear it has been done a year or two later.

But I am pursuing surgery.

Why?

Because I have chosen to live the rest of my life as a woman, and a woman does not have a penis.

Society believes gender is absolute; much of the society around me would have me remain a man. Those people think it would be so much easier for them if I remained a man.

By entering into the RLT, I am refusing to accept society's dictates. I am saying that I have a right to live the life I choose, not the life society chose for me based on a chromosomal count.

When I have the SRS, the effect will also be to deny society's petty definition of what is right or wrong.

However, and this is important, that is not the reason for my SRS.

I am not going through the RLT or SRS to teach society anything.

I am doing this for myself. Society can take any lesson it wishes from my life.

SRS will just be a footnote to my RLT; it will simply bring part of my body in line with my self image.

Much of society will not even know when I have the surgery.

But I will.

Kristin

• • •

This exceptional narrative is a cautionary tale for therapists who presuppose that they must parse for individual pathology, while ignoring the social pathology that emerges in bas relief. Gender conditions arouse intense societal anger and even abuse.

As we have seen, children with gender conditions learn, early on, to hide parts of the self that have been deemed unacceptable. In the genesis of what Sullivan termed the pseudoself, the transgendered youth tries to wall off the authentic self (the bad me), and to seek acceptance via stereotypical, but low-interest activities (the good me). The need for acceptance, coupled with a desire to appear "normal," combine to stunt identity development. Like the Bonsai tree that is dwarfed in infancy, the transgendered person is unable to pursue self-actualization, owing to the foreshortened venues for psychic growth.

It is quite common for clients to describe "faking" ejaculation, an exuberance for sports, or other behaviors, to fit in with the implicit social demands in a given situation. This betrayal of the true self often manifests as an intense preoccupation with pleasing others, not disappointing people, being overly apologetic, or otherwise self-deprecating.

One transsexual client told of keeping a written log of jokes on hand at all times. This way he felt "Patrick" could always entertain people and be socially accepted without having to engage in spontaneous conversation.

Perhaps the most obvious area in which the transgendered individual attempts to gain acceptance, while negotiating the self, is in intimate relationships. Kristen aptly described her multiple marriages as attempts at being "saved" from her gender "longings."

Sometimes the transgendered person will confide his/her cross-gender identification to the spouse before marriage. If the relationship proceeds despite this disclosure, the transgendered individual feels relief, bordering on euphoria. This comfort may be short-lived, as many spouses who initially confer acceptance may later withdraw from the relationship, as discomfort increases. Often they capitulate to evidence indicating that harmless cross-dressing is escalating and their fear that it will lead to sex change (Brown, 1994).

Not surprisingly, many transgendered individuals choose not to reveal their gender issues to a potential mate. For some, this is a seemingly prudent way to avoid what they fear will be flat-out abandonment. Others mistakenly believe that the marriage will put an end to the gender desires, so it is unnecessary to even broach the subject. When the gender dysphoria is later discovered or revealed, the spouse's anger at having been "lied to" and "betrayed" can add to the feelings of guilt and unworthiness in the transgendered individual.

One transgendered client dated his wife for six years before their marriage. He describes their premarital relationship as "wonderful . . . we were really like best friends." In his desire to be absolutely candid with her, he told her that he often cross-dressed and even had feelings of wishing he were a woman. His girlfriend seemed understanding. After this six-year courtship, this individual went to a counselor to explore these gender issues and make some decisions as to how to live his life. The counselor knew nothing about cross-dressing behavior or gender conditions, and after four sessions the young man left treatment.

Feeling confused and conflicted, he married his girlfriend in a June wedding. For two months after the wedding things seemed okay. He assumed the gender role of "husband" and tried to convince himself that this was working. However, he grew noticeably depressed. His spouse and friends were concerned about him. He was totally uninterested in sexual relations with his wife. Finally, he once again opened up to his wife about his feelings, in the fifth month of their marriage: "Remember the feelings I told you about before, my wanting to be a woman?" His wife replied that she thought he had "worked through" that in therapy; she moved out the very next day, never to see him again.

Guilt over the "damage," or perceived damage, done to others is often expressed in therapeutic situations and thwarts realistic decision-making. In a study of 262 patients, Schaefer and Wheeler (1995) identified guilt as underlying a host of psychological problems facing the gender-variant individual. This guilt about one's condition leads to the formation of defensive maneuvers and compensatory strategies, as a means of "undoing" and atonement.

In order to understand the profound toxicity of this gender guilt to the development of identity, it is essential to understand the emotion, or more precisely the affect, of *shame*. Donald Nathanson is a psychiatrist who has written extensively on the affect system, and particularly the affect of shame. Referring to Sullivan as the founder of American psychiatry, Nathanson superimposes affect, biologically wired mechanisms that are triggered in response to conditions that recur throughout life, atop the phenomenological experiences of self-in-relation-to-others, which Sullivan outlined.

So, return to the gender-confused child who, after age two, is capable of cognitively reflecting that parts of the self are not valued, e.g., contrary exhibitions of gender. These experiences form the "bad me." On the other hand, behaviors that elicit praise and acceptance comprise the "good me." According to Nathanson, "in the simplest possible terms, 'good me' equals pride, and 'bad me' equals shame" (1992). This linkage is not just a cognitive appraisal that certain behaviors are disapproved of, but evokes a biological assemblage of physiological sequelae that is scripted into the human circuitry. The affect shame throws the organism into a painful state of inner tension. It interferes with neocortical cognition, causes the head to drop, eyes to turn downward, the face to undergo vasodilatation (blush), and a brief incapacity to speak.

But more importantly, shame has one characteristic that is unlike any other affect—it has the ability to act as an attenua-

tor system. As the organism becomes able to assemble perceptions into patterns, and compare patterns with other patterns
stored in long-term memory, mismatched patterns that appear
in the midst of interest or enjoyment, reduce the positive affect
that was operational a moment before:

> Shame affect is a highly painful mechanism that operates
> to pull the organism away from whatever might interest it
> or make it content. Shame is painful in direct proportion
> to the degree of positive affect it limits. . . . The specific
> "feel" of shame is that of an impediment to something we
> had wanted or enjoyed or which excited or pleased us.
> Although the affect is triggered initially by chance occur-
> rence, later we learn new triggers for shame. The more
> information we can absorb, the more functions that can be
> handled by the ever-evolving brain of our species, the
> more these triggers for shame can be found. (Nathanson,
> 1992, pp. 138, 139)

Shame can interfere with any activity. It operates to reduce
not only interest–excitement, but also enjoyment–joy, the affects
that make people fun, charming, and engaging. Nathanson
advises psychotherapists who encounter clients who appear
lacking in vitality to "look first for nearness to shame."

Few experiences are as painful as the feeling of being deserv-
ing of rejection. Over time, the incorporation of shame affect
and other affects of rejection, such as disgust, are solidified.
This amalgamation of painful affect and negative self-appraisal
acts as an instrument to isolate the self. Shame in such wise
molds character by causing the individual to avoid contact lest
something be exposed and trigger shame. We have seen this system at work in the formation of the identity of the gender-variant child as he or she progresses developmentally toward preadolescence and accumulates shame-based self-perceptions.

Thus shame ravages the self. It concerns Nathanson that so
little is understood about the nature of shame and the develop-

ment of psychopathology. Few therapists are aware of how deeply shame influences the entire character structure. For example:

> It seems obvious to anybody who has studied shame that the so-called "borderline illness" is little more than an exaggerated result of the interference in development to be expected when a child encounters severe impediments to positive affect while learning to be independent. "Borderlines" are shame-bound people loaded with diss-mell and self-disgust . . . a large part of the time spent in therapy is devoted to meticulous reconstruction of life events made painful by shame. The importance of shame in these cases is rivaled by few clinical conditions encountered in the practice of psychotherapy. (p. 183)

Kristen's journey is an erudite narrative of the insidious and pervasive nature of shame-based depression. Surely, gender-conflicted people do indeed rival, if not surpass, other individuals in terms of the extent of shame-damage that has affixed itself to the self, defying triumphant living.

8

Effective Psychotherapy

I go away for several weeks of the year, taking the role of a woman. My rule is that I don't dress within 60 miles of the parish . . . there is, however, a real joy of being yourself for a while. I try to grab time when people are out to care for my wardrobe. At other times I cry myself to sleep. Not being the one you want to be and appear to be, you are never at ease with yourself.
— A Vicar in the Church of England,
from the *Sunday Times*, London, 1998

Case one: Susan R. has had a private practice in Albuquerque, New Mexico, for three years. Her clients are primarily adolescents and adults, although she does counsel couples. One day, a man phoned and made an appointment, stating that he resided in Montana, but was in town for business purposes. Susan recalls that he was a large, imposing figure, with a full, heavy, beard. She was totally unprepared for his startling disclosure: He was having difficulties with his wife because she had discovered his cross-dressing. He went on to describe to the counselor that, try as he might, he could never give up his need to dress. He had told his wife "this is just part of who I am."

Case two: Dr. J. has been working weekly with a married couple for two years. Although there seems to be a strong connection between the spouses, and an overall sense of good will, their frequent arguments, often about money, are eroding the relationship. On their most recent visit, the husband reveals what he has previously been reluctant to tell Dr. J.: He wears female undergarments and hosiery beneath his work clothes. His wife seems relieved that her husband has finally broached this secret, humiliating issue.

Case three: In a rural area of Illinois, a man who has "cut himself" is being treated by emergency room staff. Prior to discharge, a staff psychiatrist has been called to consult, before the patient can be sent home with a prescription for antibiotics. The psychiatrist finds the man sobbing softly. He reveals that he wants to be a woman and has cut his testicles in an attempt to blockade the production of testosterone.

Case four: A court-appointed psychologist has been asked to evaluate a man who is seeking to have his birth certificate changed. At first, the psychologist is baffled as to why this man would be embroiled in a controversy about legal documents. The young man explains that he was born female, and although he has had hormonal treatments and mastectomy, he cannot afford the genital surgery. The state in which he was born will not alter his birth certificate unless he can provide a notarized verification, from the surgeon, attesting that said sex reassignment surgery has been completed. Failure to do so will jeopardize his ability to attain a passport and travel to Europe on business. His employer does not know of his prior female history, and he fears he will lose his job should this become common knowledge. At the time of his visit with the psychologist, his anxiety is approaching panic proportions.

The above case examples are just a few of a multitude of scenarios in which mental health professionals make contact with transgendered persons in need of services. As these cases indicate, the caregiver who is unfamiliar with gender conditions is usually at a loss as to what treatments, if any, are appropriate in a given situation.

In fact, it is safe to predict that every mental health care provider will encounter at least one transgendered "client" at some point in his or her professional life. Even if they refer to a colleague more experienced in this area, it behooves professionals to understand the nature of gender conditions so that they can act fittingly and expediently. Therapists who lack experience but opt to work with transgendered clients bear the professional obligation of seeking consultation or supervision from a gender specialist.

In an attempt to address these issues facing both consumers and professionals, a group of care providers who specialize in the treatment of gender conditions, members of the Harry Benjamin International Gender Dysphoria Association, drafted the *Standards of Care* in 1979 (see Appendix A). The major purpose of the document was to present professional consensus about psychiatric, medical, and surgical management of gender conditions—referred to as "triadic treatment"—and the parameters within which professionals could offer services to individuals. *The Standards of Care* were revised in 1980, 1981, 1990, and 1998.

The *Standards* mandated a prescribed length of psychological treatment for transgendered persons who requested medical services. Contrary hormones and surgical procedures could be obtained only after said psychological treatment and endorsement. This mandated care brought thousands of transsexuals to mental health practitioners to ensure compliance with the *Standards*. This further pointed to the inadequacy of caregivers to provide the sought-after services. Regrettably, some mental health practitioners seized the role of "gatekeeper" to financially exploit a vulnerable population.

It is not simply ignorance about the condition that renders so few professionals able and willing to work with transgendered clients. One overarching dilemma is the cognitive dissonance that is triggered by the very nature of the condition. Most people process information visually. The somatic changes in the client, often dramatic, provide perceptual information that cognitively competes with other beliefs operating simultaneously in consciousness. As seemingly paradoxical bits of information vie for cognitive processing, dissonance is produced, derailing closure. In other words, one must be cognitively flexible to work with individuals who undergo physical change that runs counter to deeply ingrained, bedrock beliefs. Such flexibility requires a goodly amount of personal plasticity on the part of the clinician.

Consider this situation: A client called a psychologist who worked at a mental health agency and spoke to her on the phone. He related that he had a "gender identity disorder" and was seeking treatment. He asked her if she were willing and able to work with him. The psychologist assured him that she could provide counseling and they set a mutually agreeable time. When the pleasant sounding "man" she had spoken to arrived at her office with long, polished nails and wearing earrings, the psychologist appeared visibly jarred, and told him he had to see a psychiatrist who specialized in "sexual problems."

Therapist flexibility extends to providing an atmosphere for therapy that is comfortable for the client, including private bathroom space and waiting room areas that are reasonably secluded. Therapists should anticipate that sometimes clients will appear for sessions "dressed" and at other times, perhaps if coming from work, will present conventionally. It is also helpful to arrange for parking situations that allow clients to walk safely and comfortably to the therapist's office in cross-gender presentations.

Another obstacle for professionals has to do with theoretical ideologies. As we have seen, effective psychotherapy with transgendered clients flies in the face of much of the conventional pedagogy intrinsic to counseling and psychotherapy. It requires the clinician to shift paradigms.

There is little room, if any, for example, for psychoanalytic dogma or traditional psychoanalytically oriented treatment among the transgendered population seeking services. Similarly, practitioners who rely heavily on cognitive or behavioral strategies to promote change will experience frustration at what has been referred to as the "transsexual imperative"—the need to transform oneself despite rational or measured cognitive interference.

More successful will be those practitioners who are humanistically or existentially oriented in theory. They will resonate with the transsexual's movement toward self-definition. They are also at an advantage in that they are accustomed to acknowledging and affirming phenomenological and experiential states that are ego-dystonic. They may, however, experience discomfort with the more directive role that they will be called upon to play, for successful therapeutic interventions require the clinician to operate within a holistic framework and to be educator, therapist, and often, advocate.

So little is understood about gender conditions that very often even the client is at a loss to comprehend the feelings that run so deeply. Clinicians must, first and foremost, educate the clients about the nature of the condition for which they are seeking treatment. They must explain that the condition appears to be lifelong, that no cure exists, and that the client did nothing to create this condition. It is also important for the individual to understand that, just like many things in life, interest in cross-gender expression may well vary in intensity, or periodically remit, over the course of a lifetime. Simply educating the client, sharing what information is known about the condition, has the effect of attenuating the shame the gender dysphoric person internalizes.

It is also crucial that the therapist convey a deep respect for the client and the exploration being embarked upon. Nothing will serve to sunder rapport with more certainty than the refusal to address the client by the client's preferred name and with matching pronouns. This author recalls imploring a psychiatrist to address a male-to-female transsexual living full-time as female by the feminine name she was using. When I suggested that the psychiatrist be flexible, he responded that his idea of being flexible meant "working evenings"!

Oftentimes, therapists are unaware that sexual orientation can be fluid and that individuals who take hormones and transition may experience a shift in preferences. A therapist was very concerned about a high-functioning physician who had previously been married and fathered children when, after transition, this person began to date men. The therapist was under the impression that this was evidence of some severe, underlying pathology, rather than an example of the fluidity of sexual orientation that is typical in this population.

Respect and empathy act in tandem to provide clients with permission to grow and learn while accommodating to their new gender role. The therapist who displays such attitudes and incorporates them into the therapeutic process provides a counter-shaming experience for the client, so essential for successful life transition.

This validation by the therapist may be viewed by some as akin to the transference phenomenon, in that it is reparative and reminiscent of the primordial parent-child relationship. But it is quite unlike what is typically described as transference. The therapist does not rely on unconscious material to be offered as grist for the therapeutic mill. Instead, the therapist is proactive in creating an alliance with the client and is willing to be an active, even nurturing participant in such a venture.

One frequently encountered question that counselors raise is the issue of *timing* in the therapeutic work, as this case illustrates: A counselor at a mental health clinic in a small town has been treating a client for four years. He initially presented with problems relating to alcohol use, marital problems, cross-dressing, and job stress. The counselor has worked hard to address the alcohol and marital problems, often seeing the spouse conjointly. Whenever the client brings up his cross-dressing and the distress it is causing him, the counselor tells him that they will deal with that issue "last" after they have addressed these more "important," pressing problems.

A colleague in a large metropolitan area related a similar story: A client she had been following requested a referral to a family therapist. As it happened, a nationally known expert practiced nearby. The client and his wife entered treatment with great optimism, given the credentials and fame of the therapist. At the first session, the client stated that they were there because of his cross-dressing and its impact on the family. The issue was a "hot potato," for it was never acknowledged by the therapist, or ever mentioned again, even after a year of regular family sessions.

Some therapists incorrectly assume that gender problems always arise from early sexual abuse. When clients talk about not wanting to have partners touch their genitals, such therapists conclude "suspicions confirmed." Dislike of the body and genitals is characteristic of gender dysphoria and does not invariably imply early sexual abuse. In cases where there is a history of sexual abuse, the gender identity issues must still be given therapeutic priority.

Gender problems are so central to formation, regulation, and defense of self that they should always be addressed and acknowledged at the very outset of treatment. Many other seemingly intractable problems the client faces (including some Axis I and Axis IV factors) "dissolve" when the client confronts the gender issue with a trusted and supportive ally. Counselors who avoid dealing with the gender issue echo the client's unease, which amplifies shame.

Another problem counselors face is a tendency to fall victim to stereotypical gender biases or binary, "either-or" categorical thinking. One client, a 53-year-old married man who was in the process of acknowledging his lifelong feelings of gender incongruity, was told by a therapist that he "must decide whether he wanted to remain living as a man or have surgery." Such reductionistic messages serve to create additional negative affect in the client and to rob the client of the opportunity to generate and select options for comfortably integrating cross-gender identities.

Similarly, some individuals have been "counseled out of" needed treatments by therapists who told them they were "too short to be a man," "too tall to be a woman," or that they would never be "attractive" in their preferred gender!

As Schaefer and Wheeler (1995) emphasize, effective therapy involves an appreciation for the uniqueness of each transgendered person and the genesis of goals that mesh with the particulars of the psychosocial context of that client's life. Some of the options for cross-gender expression are intermittent or partial and can include inconspicuous cross-dressing or cross-dressing *under* male or female clothing, living socially in the opposite gender but working in the assigned gender, removal of facial and body hair in the male-to-female, increasing muscular development in the female-to-male, facial and other cosmetic surgeries such as hair weaves and breast implants—indeed the entire panoply of impressive cosmetic interventions—and periodic use of hormones. Many combinations of strategies emerge in theory and in practice, and clients should be encouraged to consider and pursue serviceable alternatives, rather than regarding sex-reassignment surgery as the only appropriate option.

In addition to understanding the range of choices the client may opt for, the therapist must encourage the client to appreciate that choices can change as responsibilities, finances, or other vicissitudes of life change (Blanchard, 1994). Options that are not available or prudent at one point in time may be more attainable and viable at a later date. For example, a 45-year-old male-to-female lived unhappily as a man while he battled the federal government in a patent suit. Once the suit settled, he had the freedom and funds to pursue the longed for gender reassignment.

It is not altogether uncommon for clients to abruptly terminate therapy after several productive sessions. In such cases clients tend to leave phone messages or write letters advising the therapist that they are not returning. Quite often the message will state that they are no longer having "a gender problem" or, as one client wrote, "I know that my cross-dressing is over . . . gender will never be a problem in my life again." Since denial has been employed in the past, albeit unsuccessfully, the client may revert to this protective strategy again. The therapist can head off this defensive maneuver by educating clients early on that denial is never a healthy option for living with the condition. When clients learn how devastating denial is, they will connect previous attempts to deny the condition to depression, hopelessness, misguided decision-making, possible suicide attempts, or other evidence of emotional havoc in their personal history.

Sadly, sometimes the pressure to avoid honest acknowledgment of the gender issue comes from without, not from within. Paula, a 63-year-old male-to-female transsexual, received the following letter from her adult children via registered mail:

> *Dear Paul,*
>
> *We will pray for your conversion to the Lord, and a return to manhood. Until a full return is made to your masculinity, we consider you to have severed your relationships with all of us.*
>
> *Until you find a personal relationship with Christ, which we believe to be the only way to facilitate a complete turn-around in your life, our families require that you no longer have any contact with any of us—adult or minor.*

To be "shorn from the herd," as Nathanson puts it, is shame in its most horrifying visage. How can the therapist ameliorate the toxicity of this cognitive and affective trauma, which is exacerbated by the accumulation of experiences of shame, and its offspring humiliation and guilt, in the affect system? By demonstrating what Carl Rogers termed "unconditional positive regard," by creating a sanctuary of safety, and by offering empathic verbal responses, therapy acts like a tourniquet to siphon off the toxic venom of shame and soothe the pain of feeling loathsome and rejected. Nathanson describes these indispensable elements of effective psychotherapy:

> Essential is a basic empathic stance that shows you know and feel the other person's pain. This must be verbalized in a distinctive manner that indicates some sort of joining with the patient. Central to treatment is the understanding that the patient, stuck alone in the shame experience, is unable to return to normal interpersonal interaction unaided. The empathic therapist is able to enter the patient's pain at this deeply personal level, join with it, and then pull them both out of the humiliation. . . . *Therapeutic passivity—the decision to remain silent—* . . . *will always magnify shame because it confirms the patient's affect-driven belief that isolation is justified.* (1992, pp. 324, 325) (italics in original)

Although it is a cherished canon in psychotherapy that the therapist allow the client to find his or her own solutions to problems, working with the transgendered often requires violating this precept. Advice-giving, anathema to traditional treatment, is often essential to helping the client live safely and comfortably. Transitioning on the job while protecting employment and maintaining coworker support, disclosure and maintenance of family relationships, how and when to discuss gender variance with one's children, and sharing choices with religious or spiritual leaders and communities are a few examples of the many critical issues transgendered clients face. Recommendations by the counselor, gleaned from experience and knowledge of existing resources, can help clients resolve interpersonal conflict, maintain steady income streams, and find satisfaction in daily living.

The therapist need not operate alone in this regard, for support groups and conventions are widely available to share collective experience and provide support. These groups can also furnish resources for vendors of wardrobe, makeup, wigs, electrolysis, breast-binders for female-to-males, or other accouterments necessary for cross-gender presentation, as well as recommendations for cosmetic surgeons, health care, and legal advisors. Additionally, social outings organized by support groups afford opportunities for experimentation and refinement of personal style and presentation while breaking down isolation and building new relationships that enhance self-worth.

Female-to-Male Transsexualism

Clinicians unaccustomed to working with female-to-male transsexuals may mistakenly assume that the issues in this population mirror the issues of male-to-female transsexuals. More obscured from public view, and less often the subject of media sensationalism, these individuals differ in significant ways.

Those who work extensively with this population note that they are psychologically better adjusted than their male-to-female counterparts. These clinical observations and anecdotal accounts have been documented, and there appears to be substantially fewer Axis II disorders in this population. Likewise, female-to-male transsexuals more commonly have stable partnerships, are more likely to engage in monogamous behavior, and are, overall, better integrated socially than male-to-female-transsexuals (De Cuypere, Janes, & Rubens, 1995; Fleming, MacGowan, & Costos, 1985; Levine, 1980; Steiner &

Bernstein, 1981). Moreover, these aforementioned patterns are true pre- and postoperatively, which is significant because female-to-male surgical outcomes are anatomically less precise.

Kockott and Fahrener (1988) reported that female-to-male transsexuals more often had close ties to both parents and siblings, were more relationship-oriented, more socially integrated even prior to beginning treatment for gender-reassignment, and more sexually satisfied than male-to-female transsexual counterparts.

While the basis for these differences remains unclear, perhaps the answer lies in the arena of early interpersonal and cultural forces that impact on self-formation. In Western society, "tomboy" behavior is not only acceptable but often a source of parental pride, unlike sissy behavior in boys, which is socially abhorrent. Young girls who are uncomfortable with burgeoning femininity can adopt gender-neutral presentations that are unremarkable during childhood. While parents may experience disappointment or chagrin when their young daughters eschew female clothing, the struggles are quartered within the family, not the community of reference or society at large.

Compare, then, the experience of a ten-year-old girl who insists on wearing jeans and sweatshirts and adores soccer to that of the ten-year-old boy who prefers dresses and jewelry and adores Barbie®. In the former case, such predilections leave the self largely intact. In the latter instance, layer upon layer of shame are continuously constructed, thwarting healthy personality formation, accurate self-appraisal, and interpersonal success. Personality disorders are enduring, characterological ways of thinking, feeling, and behaving that are rooted in childhood. The lack of shame inflicted on the young female-to-male may lessen the likelihood of personality disorders in adulthood.

For the female-to-male, puberty, particularly menstruation, signals the end of gender ambiguity and creates a crisis. Many female-to-males recall the trauma of the onset of menses and their ensuing dysthymia. The development of breasts is the first visible ego-dystonic feature of body morphology that requires psychological accommodation. Attempts to remain androgynous after the emergence of adolescence will cause these individuals to be labeled as "lesbian," inferring that their gender nonconformity is a sign of sexual preference, rather than an issue of gender identity.

This issue often remains a stumbling block to early self-identification in the female-to-male transsexuals, for often they accept this ill-fitting label and remain ensconced in lesbian relationships and communities. Lesbian partners, and sometimes lesbian therapists, may wittingly or unwittingly discourage exploration that leads to the acknowledgment of tenaciously held feelings of masculinity and the "discovery" of a concealed identity.

For the subgroup of female-to-male transsexuals who are sexually attracted to men (Coleman, Bockting, & Gooren, 1993), there is much pressure initially to try to live as women, which legitimizes their sexual preference. Some of these individuals marry men in early adulthood, and some even bear children, before concluding that the issue they have been wrestling with is not one of sexuality but of their own gender identity. When they do transition, they live successfully as "gay transmen."

Therapists who are sensitive to developmental and social forces that collude in keeping female-to-male identities hidden will be better able to meet the needs of this group of people and to assist them with attaining desired medical treatments. Bilateral mastectomy and masculinizing hormones are the most commonly sought interventions, and procuring these objectives is often the impetus for entering treatment.

Sometimes, the difficulties in procuring these treatments and the determination to surmount obstacles require Herculean measures, as in the following case:

Ricardo was born in Bolivia some thirty years ago and named Rita by the loving parents who gave birth to her, their second daughter. Both girls were raised similarly, but Rita never played with dolls, ironed with mother, or for that matter took an interest in any feminine activities. As the girls grew, Rita began to confide in her mother that she wished she was a boy and dreamt of changing into a boy. Her mother, a kind and educated woman, encouraged her to pursue the athletic interests and nontraditional hobbies she was fond of. As Rita approached puberty she spent more and more time alone. Often, she would remain locked in her room drawing comics, reading, or writing in a journal.

When puberty arrived, Rita's body changed and she began to experience intense anxiety. Often, she was so immobilized by fear that she would be unable to accompany her mother to the market. Finally, it was determined that she would see a psychiatrist. Rita had grown increasingly withdrawn and depressed during the early teenage years, and she was placed on both antidepressants and antianxiety drugs.

The drugs were effective in restoring some stability to Rita, and she tried to adjust to life in her traditional South American culture, a life that required stringent conformity to restrictive gender roles. As Rita approached early adulthood, she did what all normal young females in the society did: She married. Rita chose as her husband the boy who had always been her best pal, the friend with whom she was able to play sports and pursue other common interests.

The marriage was brief and unsatisfying for both spouses, who divorced and returned to their previous status of being "best friends." By this time, Rita's psychiatrist had confirmed diagnostically what Rita had known all along: Rita suffered from the rare condition known as transsexualism. No treatments were available.

Rita's revulsion at her body, specifically her breasts, which she bound, and her monthly menses, led her to pursue all possible venues for transformation. By extreme cunning, she was able to convince a surgeon that abdominal pain and irregular bleeding necessitated a hysterecto-my. Next, she located a plastic surgeon who agreed to do "breast reduction," which gave the patient a masculine appearing chest and yet left the surgeon in no personal jeopardy.

While the removal of these secondary sex characteristics provided great comfort for Rita, she was not satisfied to live as "half man, half woman." Her mother, sympathetic to her plight and wanting only an end to her child's mis-ery, researched treatment for the condition. She concluded that it was necessary for her child to go to the States, where she could obtain masculinizing hormones.

Mother and daughter exchanged tearful good-byes and Rita left for the States on what would be a perilous trip. For bureaucratic reasons, she was detained at immigra-tions and thrown in jail. After several terrifying days of incarceration, Rita was released into the custody of a South American lawyer who agreed to send her home if she would pay an outrageous sum of money to him for "bail." Rita's mother begrudgingly exchanged thousands of dollars for Rita's safe return.

After the disastrous trip to the States, Rita plummeted into depression. There was no hope of ever becoming the man she was inside, and she felt doomed to living a mean-ingless, inauthentic existence. Her mother was frightened by the depths of Rita's despair. In the following months, Rita's sister, Eva, gave birth to her second child. Family life was busy for Eva, who owned a small farm along with her husband. One day, Eva approached Rita and suggested the following plan: Rita could have Eva's passport, assume Eva's identity, and remain forever in the United States. As Eva, she could obtain permanent visitor status. Eva herself had no desire to ever travel outside of her homeland and was not in need of these documents.

Once again Rita said good-bye to her family and left Bolivia. She arrived unceremoniously in the United States via Miami and then traveled on to Chicago. Rita lived with an aunt and worked at minimum wage in a factory for three long years, trying to adopt to a new culture, learn a new language, and live among strangers. Finally, she accumulated enough funds to begin the long-awaited hormonal therapy.

Almost immediately things improved for Rita. She discovered that with hormones she felt better—less anxious and depressed—and was able to discontinue psychotropic medication. Soon the inevitable physical changes occurred, and Rita politely asked coworkers to call him Ricardo.

Recently, Ricardo married a young woman he works with at the factory. His mother came from Bolivia to attend the wedding and appeared radiant at the festive event. Eva was unable to attend.

Children With Gender-Variant Behavior

Treatment modalities for gender-variant children, or children who meet the *DSM-IV* diagnostic criteria for gender identity disorder of childhood (302.6) remain controversial. As parents, grandparents, or other caretakers make the contact with the helping professional, it is imperative that the counselor distinguish *gender nonconformity,* in which children display behavior that is inconsistent with reigning cultural stereotypes, from *gender dysphoria*—a distressing and profound upheaval in the child's sense of identity.

There is a widespread belief that these children also frequently have separation anxiety (DiCeglie, Sturge, & Sutton, 1998). Reduction and management of such anxiety or other coexisting behavioral or affective difficulties are a primary and realistic treatment goal. The *Standards of Care* specify that professionals who offer assessment or therapeutic interventions in children or adolescents with gender conflicts should be trained in developmental psychopathology and be generally competent in assessment and treatment of children and adolescents.

Not all children who meet the criteria for gender identity disorder will evolve into adults with transgendered identities (Davenport, 1986; Di Ceglie et al., 1998; Zucker & Bradley,

1995). Therapeutic interventions must be aimed at working with parents and siblings to maintain family stability. Parents need not only support but also mundane strategies for managing the child's behavior in a way that is nonshaming and does not erode self-esteem. Family and marital therapy may be part of a constellation of treatment venues, based on assessment. Follow-up of these children is particularly crucial, as developmental changes occur physically, emotionally, and sexually, requiring reassessment and reconfiguration of treatment goals.

Dealing with children who exhibit gender-variant behavior is a challenge for even the most loving parents and experienced educators. Parents must be warned to exercise extreme caution in engaging the services of professionals who offer aversion-type therapies or radical, unproven methods that purport to rid the child of cross-gendered behaviors or desires.

In the past few years, parents of such children have banded together to advocate on behalf of their children and support one another. These support groups can be extremely valuable, particularly for families living in areas without child specialists.

Postsurgical Psychotherapy

The questions most frequently asked regarding transsexualism have to do with the particulars of surgery and postoperative outcomes. There appears to be a fascination and an endless appetite for details of conversion techniques. The media has fed this hunger by portraying the most sensational scenarios of human drama that feature transsexuals. These stories have all the essentials of maintaining high viewer interest, as they are both provocative and visually compelling (replete with "before" and "after" photographs). Unfortunately, such media portrayals do little to elucidate the true nature of gender conditions. Most often they are merely exploitative. If there is an educative purpose, it is to remind us that, in an age of political correctness, it is still okay to mock the transgendered.

A favored media-propagated myth is the notion that transsexuals undergo horrible, mutilating surgery, to their everlasting regret. One can see why this oft-portrayed plot appeals: It reinforces the stereotype that transsexuals are deranged individuals who, for some bizarre reason, think that they would be better off embracing a different "lifestyle." Then they awaken from the anesthesia, appalled by the horror visited upon them. Such absurdity apparently makes for good television programming!

In truth, outcome studies of postoperative results are quite consistent and point to high satisfaction levels with surgical reassignment (Jarrar, Wolff, & Weidner, 1996; Kuiper & Cohen-Kettenis, 1988; Lief & Hubschman, 1993; Mate-Kole, Freschi, & Robin, 1990; Pfafflin, 1992; Rakic, Starcevic, Maric, & Kelin, 1996; Snaith, Tarsh, & Reid, 1993). Satisfaction is largely dependent on successful surgeries performed by competent, experienced surgeons (Botzer, Vehrs, & Biber, 1993; Eldh, Berg, & Gustafson, 1997; Ross & Need, 1989). By 1980, over 1,000 patients had been operated upon in the United States. Only a very small number expressed regrets after surgery or committed suicide. One estimate is that about 2% of the male-to-female transsexuals and only 0.5% of female-to-male postoperative transsexuals attempt suicide. More than seventy follow-up studies have been carried out concluding that reassignment surgery is indeed therapeutic (Kuiper & Cohen-Kettenis, 1995).

While there is consensus of opinion about surgical outcomes—patients report almost unanimous satisfaction with the procedures—there is evidence that many individuals experience psychosocial difficulties post-surgery. In a 1995 study, researchers conducted extended personal interviews with male-to-female patients who had undergone surgery (Lazer, Benet, Rehman, Schaefer, & Melman). This group of patients was highly satisfied with the functional and cosmetic results of the surgery. However, most of the patients expressed some degree of disappointment with their postsurgical social adjustment. For some there were unexpected problems in acclimating to the new gender role. Often, this involved concerns about forming intimate relationships, lack of confidence in dating or courting behaviors, or fears about how and when to reveal one's previous gender status. A 1998 study of female-to-male transsexuals who had phalloplasty found that, although there was greater satisfaction in genital appearance postoperatively, operated subjects showed higher depression scores on an assessment instrument than non-operated counterparts (Barret). Perhaps this reflects unrealistic expectations that precede phalloplasty.

One client came to counseling stating that, although she had been operated on twenty years ago, she still was having difficulties in interpersonal relationships. This client had difficulty making friends with other women, yet yearned for female companionship. Even though it had been two decades since her reassignment, she perceived gaps in her knowledge of what it meant to live successfully in her "new" gender.

It is wholly understandable that for a person who has dreamed of living an authentic and physically consonant life after struggling with incongruent gender, there may be disappointment when certain realities collide with fantasies about life after surgery. While the *Standards of Care* require treatment prior to surgery, there has been little attention paid to the psychological needs of people postoperatively.

Some gender specialists have found group therapy to be a very efficacious and affordable venue for postoperative clients. Not only does the group offer support, but it also provides a social network that can transcend the limits of the therapy session and reduce isolation. Within the context of the group, clients can work on intimacy issues, self-esteem, career concerns, or other issues that may have been preempted by surgery.

Clinicians should make themselves available to postoperative clients who want continued support or psychotherapy (Lothstein & Levine, 1981). It is important for clinicians to understand the issues, often mundane, that challenge the postoperative client. It is equally important to understand the process of adaptation—the regressive and progressive components—that merge as clients accommodate to new and evolving identities.

Treatment Obstacles

Given that the transsexual has been largely invalidated or misdiagnosed by the discipline of psychology, procuring services and treatments has often seemed as difficult as the proverbial gathering of grapes from thorns. For many, the only viable options were black-market hormones and surgery in Casablanca, Morocco.

In recent years, buoyed by research that is nonpathologizing and a solid network of support groups, consumers have become increasingly proactive in the regulation of care delivered. It is common for consumers to attend professional meetings, offer input on revisions to the *Standards of Care*, renounce the inclusion of gender identity disorders in the *DSM*, or work to change legislative statutes to protect transgendered persons from discrimination and violence.

This newly formed alliance notwithstanding, and although sensitivity, respect, and empathy have been heralded as essential qualities in the therapist, the truth is that there is often a mutual mistrust that covertly or overtly sabotages optimal therapist-client relations. Therapists often distrust the client's history or self-description, fearing they are being misled or lied to by one who is desperate to obtain hormones and/or surgery. This fear may be fueled by the knowledge that some individuals have appeared in the media claiming that they lied to the therapist to gain approval for surgery and were inappropriately surgically reassigned, with disastrous consequences. Or perhaps the client has threatened, or attempted, autocastration. Such concerns have led some therapists to undertake independent fact-finding or verification of particulars of clients' history and authenticity of documents, or to delay approval of medical procedures.

Similarly, clients often approach therapy with mistrust, fearing that desired treatments will be denied or postponed while they jump through seemingly endless "hoops" that the therapist fabricates. Sadly, many frustrated individuals have spent much time and money "educating" uninformed general mental health practitioners about the condition. One client related that he would see his psychiatrist weekly, bringing in a different book or article at every visit, to educate the physician. After a number of such visits, the psychiatrist concluded that the condition was "valid" and asked the patient which hormones, and at what dosages, were appropriate to administer!

It is useful to talk with clients about their previous therapy experiences. Prior negative experiences may contribute to mistrust of the therapist or doubts about the usefulness of therapy. This often applies to adolescents, who may have been inaccurately labeled, drugged, or hospitalized previously, and are fearful of entering treatment again.

Not all adult clients experience distress about their transgendered identities. Many individuals have found ways to live and work with ease and do not require psychotherapeutic interventions. Therapists must be ever mindful of the goals of treatment: to help maximize success in work and in relationships, and to actualize one's full potential in life, while finding comfort in gender role and body.

9

A Multidisciplinary Approach

It took me forty-two years to discover that there is a term for a female who feels like a male. It's not "crazy" . . . it is "transgendered."
— A female-to-male transsexual

The clinical management of gender conditions requires a multidisciplinary approach (Gilbert, Winslow, Gilbert, Jordan, & Horton, 1988). Professionals often team up formally or informally to provide services for members of the transgendered community (Auge et al.,1997). Whether one works alone or finds willing colleagues within other specialties, the mental health practitioner must have a working familiarity with the other disciplines, services, and treatments that come into play.

First and foremost, the therapist must understand the rudiments of hormonal therapy for both male-to-female and female-to-male transsexuals.

Male-to-Female Hormonal Treatment

There is no universal protocol for administering contrary hormones to patients. Physicians use protocols that empirically produce the desired results, hopefully utilizing the lowest dosages consistent with feminization (Futterweit, 1998). Most often this consists of the administration of conjugated estrogens at 1.25 mg to 2.5 mg per day, or intramuscular injections of ethinyl estradiol, or transdermal estradiol patches, or some combination of the above. Progestins can be introduced after commencing hormones to stimulate breast development. Some protocols include cycling of progesterone to mimic the genetic female monthly hormonal fluctuations. Additionally, patients benefit from antiandrogenic compounds.

With the above cross-sex hormones, biologic males will realize the following desired physical changes: softening of the skin, redistribution of body fat, breast development, decrease in muscle mass, cessation of male-pattern hair loss, atrophy of the genitals, diminution of body hair, and decrease in fertility and libido. The above changes are reversible if hormones are discontinued, although breast tissue may never return to its previous configuration and changes in libido may be permanent.

Although patients sometimes become impatient with the rate of change, response varies depending on individual characteristics, tissue response, and heredity. Maximum effects are generally evident after two years of uninterrupted treatment. Giving extremely high doses to counteract a lack of progress may be counter-therapeutic, in that estrogenic compounds at such levels may break down into the precursors of testosterone, as the system attempts to maintain homeostasis. Medical risk factors also escalate when dosage levels increase beyond appropriately prescribed levels.

Most frequent and significant among the adverse reactions in this population are vascular complications, ranging from clotting to embolism, and liver abnormalities, ranging from hyperplasias to adenomas.

Hormones have psychological effects, too, most often inducing feelings of well-being in the male-to-female transsexual. Many patients do not need psychiatric medications for comorbid conditions after commencing hormones.

Physicians who administer hormones will monitor these patients closely. Initially, they will do complete physical exams, take careful medical histories, and do laboratory studies. They will do repeat laboratory studies and exams, palpating veins and otherwise carefully screening for adverse reactions. Some patients who have cardiovascular or other disease processes may not be good medical candidates for hormonal reassignment, although the use of transdermal patches has broadened treatment possibilities in patients with comorbid disease. Routine follow-up is essential for assessing health, reducing risk of complication, and verifying emotional well-being.

Patients who have genital surgery will be told to discontinue hormones three weeks prior to surgery in order to reduce the risks of coagulation crises. After removal of the testes, the postoperative hormonal regimen will reflect the necessity for lower doses. However, patients will need maintenance hormonal therapy for the remainder of their lifetimes.

Female-to-Male Hormonal Treatment

In the biological female requiring masculinization, an analogue of naturally occurring testosterone is the treatment of choice. Typically, this is administered intramuscularly, 200 mg twice monthly or 300 mg every three weeks. Testosterone patches can be used, and the transdermal system is both safe and efficacious. Some individuals have difficulty in keeping the patch adhered, however. This vehicle of administration has the added advantage of avoiding the "peaks and troughs" of intramuscular injections by providing continuous capillary absorption.

With the aforementioned hormonal injections, biological females will virilize. There will be a deepening of the voice, which is irreversible should one discontinue hormones. Initially, there will be changes in sebum production, which produces acne. Emotional changes include feelings of increased aggressiveness and increased libido. After about four months of treatment, menses will cease. Body fat will decrease in the hip area, while appetite increases and musculature develops. Clitoral enlargement ensues, and some atrophy of the breasts occurs. Body and facial hair grows, and male-pattern baldness develops.

Patients need to be monitored carefully. Vital signs such as blood pressure, heart rate, and weight should be reviewed frequently. Palpation of the liver should also be performed. Laboratory studies that should be obtained include serum testosterone, estradiol levels, and liver profiles.

Androgen therapy may exacerbate premorbid conditions such as hypertension or thrombo-embolic disease. Other side effects, similar to those in the male-to-female population, are diseases of the liver and gall bladder. Therefore, the lowest possible doses of testosterone consistent with virilization should be utilized. An important component to evaluation is the patient's feedback concerning body change and masculinization. Bilateral oophorectomy will allow for substantial reduction of hormonal requirements and hasten masculinization.

Alcoholism, malignancy, endocrine disorder, cardiovascular disease, liver disease, or morbid obesity may be contraindications for hormonal treatment. Physicians will weigh the benefit-risk ratio and ultimately determine the feasibility of treatments in such instances.

Sometimes patients who desire hormones will approach physicians directly, without having seen a mental health specialist, or will procure hormones on the "black market." In such cases, the clinician may be contacted by the physician, and the therapist must apprise the individual of the Standards of Care for eligibility of receiving hormones. Patients who self-medicate should be warned of the inherent dangers in this practice. The therapist who refers a patient for hormonal treatment should select a medical provider—endocrinologist or generalist—who understands the impact of hormones on all the organ systems and is experienced and comfortable working with gender-variant patients. If the clinician has a cursory knowledge of the above hormonal protocols, communication between physician and clinician will be greatly facilitated.

Hormonal treatment should only be offered to patients who understand that there are medical, psychological, and social side effects of treatment. Patients must realize that certain effects are irreversible or may create social upheaval, such as loss of employment or change in social and family relationships. Physicians will ask patients to sign informed consent statements. For adolescents, informed consent must include consent not only of the minor but of the parent or guardian as well. Prisoners who are receiving medically regulated hormones should continue such treatment during incarceration. Similarly, patients who are admitted to hospitals must continue with hormone therapy unless contraindicated for medical reasons. Without access to hormones patients can experience abrupt mood swings, as in the following example:

> Jason is a female-to-male transsexual who has fully transitioned. After a particularly stressful sequence of events, he became quite depressed and was admitted to a psychiatric hospital. Once he was hospitalized, the attending psychiatrist refused to call him "Jason" and referred to him as "Jill," although his presentation is unambiguously male. But the real danger to Jason's well-being occurred when the psychiatrist refused to allow him to take any testosterone. The sudden withdrawal of testosterone created a rapid fluctuation in the hormonal milieu, which intensified the depression, exacerbated the crisis, and caused further destabilization.

Cosmetic Surgical Procedures

Clients who wish to make changes in appearance, and those who are taking hormones in preparation for gender transition, will often seek ancillary surgical procedures to enhance authentic presentation in their chosen gender. Plastic surgery specialists offer a wide range of options for male-to-females interested in feminizing face and body via surgery.

Many patients opt for rhinoplasty, blepharoplasty, or facelift. But additionally, procedures specifically aimed at offsetting male physiognomy are available. These include "brow-shave," cheek implants, lip enhancement, chin refinement, reduction thyroid chondroplasty (tracheal shave) mandible reduction, scalp flap reduction, and hair transplant.

Body-contouring surgeries include liposuction of the waist, rib removal, and injection of fat into hips and buttocks. Augmentation mammaplasty should only be performed after maximum breast development via hormones has occurred, after about two years of continuous documented usage. Some patients opt for procedures to surgically manipulate the vocal chords and alter voice in a feminine tonal direction.

Clinicians can advise clients of surgeons who perform such surgeries and who are sensitive to the desired transformation the client is seeking. Several surgeons specialize in these procedures and will consult with clients and apprise them of how well a particular procedure will reconfigure their appearance to match their expectation.

Some patients may become so focused on having genital surgery that they postpone or abandon a desired facial surgery. Yet, for some individuals, feminization of the face brings increased social confidence and comfort in a new gender role, while genital surgery can be socially undetectable.

For female-to-males, breast reduction mammaplasty (chest-contouring) is highly desired. This procedure generally precedes any genital surgery and may be essential for living successfully in the male role. The intensity of the desire for the procedure often is dependent on breast size. Patients who are large-breasted understandably long for this procedure and should be guided to surgeons who have produced successful and aesthetic results. Some female-to-male patients may also want liposuction of areas that retain fat deposits despite hormonal intervention.

Genital Reconstructive Surgeries

Male-to-female sex-reassignment surgery consists of removal and reconfiguration of genitalia and creation of a neovagina and neoclitoris. Many surgeons routinely perform these surgeries, in the United States, and in Europe. Two methods, in general, are utilized for reassignment. The first, called the inversion technique, consists of removal of the testes and formation of a neovagina from inverted penile skin. The other method utilizes autotransplanted colon to create a vagina.

In the inversion technique, there is the advantage of not invading any other system, and thus avoiding complications of transplanted colon tissue. While the colon method allows for depth of the neovagina without the necessity of a graft, the transplanted tissue is delicate and could conceivably be damaged by rigorous intercourse. Also, excessive mucous secretions from the colon may be undesirable.

Genital surgery should include creation of a clitoris and, following labiaplasty, the result should be indistinguishable from that of the genetic female. Many patients report capacity for orgasm, and all should have adequate depth for intercourse. The patient must dilate religiously, following surgery, to assure patency of the neovagina.

There are many surgical techniques available for female-to-males; however, results do not offer precise aesthetic and functional results. Some patients will have reproductive organs removed through hysterectomy or oophorectomy.

Few patients opt for surgical phalloplasty, and those who do may have to undergo staged procedures. Although optimal results would allow for standing micturition and the ability to engage in coitus, surgery often falls short of these goals. In fact, imprecise results, prohibitive costs, and high complication rates argue against present phalloplasty procedures (Tsoi, Kok, Yeo, & Ratnam, 1995). Most female-to-males desire the ability to urinate standing, thus rendering them indistinguishable from other males in public restrooms, more than sexual ability (Hage & Bloem, 1993; Hage, Bout, Bloem, & Megens, 1993). Consequently, a more frequently performed surgery is metaoidoplasty. Here, a hormonally enlarged clitoris is freed from the vaginal hood and is transformed into a microphallus. This procedure will allow for urination while standing, but not sexual penetration. Patients must understand that the microphallus has little erectile tissue. For those patients with realistic expectations, metaoidoplasty can be a viable and satisfactory option.

Legal Issues

Clinicians should have knowledge of certain basic legal information for persons undergoing gender reassignment. Personal documents must be changed, and states vary in the requirements for doing so. For example, some states will only change a birth certificate to reflect a different gender after medical documentation is presented attesting that genital surgery has been completed. A few states will never change birth certificates, surgical conversion notwithstanding.

Patients who undergo hormonal treatment and prepare for real life experiences should carry a document stating that they are undergoing said medical procedures, following medical guidelines, and not attempting to conceal their identity for any fraudulent purpose. Such a letter may prove useful in the event that an individual is questioned by law enforcement agents.

In addition to routine legal procedures, such as name change, patients may interface with the law in other situations. Issues of divorce, child custody, and employment and labor difficulties are but a few examples. If a client can be referred to an attorney familiar with the special needs of gender clients, so much the better. If not, the clinician may be asked to help lawyers and judges understand the nature of gender conditions, so that biases or misinformation do not unnecessarily compromise legal rights.

For example, an indigent transsexual lost her minimum-wage job owing to discrimination. When she was unable to find the funds to continue with hormones, she fraudulently gained access to a few thousand dollars. She was arrested and convicted in Federal Court. Her court-appointed defense attorney strongly felt that her desperate situation and the years of frustration she had experienced dealing with her gender issues drove her to commit the crime. In his pre-sentence investigation efforts, he sought out an expert in gender conditions to evaluate the defendant and to educate the judge about how society marginalizes gender-variant individuals. The psychologist was able to explain to both attorney and judge the unique role of hormones in attenuating depression. It is hoped that the judge will take these circumstances into consideration when sentencing this individual.

Another example of the necessity of educating attorneys about transgender issues became evident in the case of Streeter vs. California State University. A preoperative male-to-female transsexual disclosed her genital status to the school prior to enrolling and was welcomed into the women's dormitory. The University later claimed that this was an error and insisted that she would have to disclose her genital status, specifically that she had a penis, to all the women in the dormitory and obtain their consent to stay; otherwise she would be evicted. Ms. Streeter did so, and obtained the written consent of every dorm resident. The school then said that wasn't enough, and Ms. Streeter was sent to live in the men's dormitory, where she had no meal privileges, and therefore no food.

The State insisted that Ms. Streeter could not live in the

women's dormitory unless she had completed sex reassignment, owing to the communal toilet and shower facilities. The attorneys engaged in an aggressive educational campaign, disabusing the State of the notion that this individual was the equivalent of a male cross-dresser, while simultaneously providing accurate information about transsexualism. This approach proved successful, and she was allowed to reside in the women's dormitory.

Collaboration with Other Mental Health Workers

Dealing with spouses, children, parents, and/or coworkers often stretches the ability of any one professional. On a team therapists may effectively undertake part of the treatment, while conferring with one another. Often, individual therapists who work with transgendered clients form networks to share talents, experiences, and referrals. Such groups provide support for clinicians. Patients can be confidentially discussed and gain from the combined input of a group of practitioners.

In some areas, a single clinician may call upon other practitioners, as the need arises, ultimately creating a network of providers who are comfortable with transgendered clients. One social worker practicing in a metropolitan area gradually educated a child psychologist about clinical aspects of transgenderism. Over a period of several years, the child psychologist treated many children who had a parent making a gender transition. This allowed her to ultimately develop ongoing therapy groups for these children. This proved to be a very fruitful way of providing therapeutic and peer support, while helping the children deal with a wide range of issues.

Similarly, some clinicians who are trained in marital and family therapy are very comfortable dealing with relationship issues. They can work in tandem with practitioners who do individual work with a given client. Therapists often collaborate with alcohol or substance abuse counselors, psychiatrists who deal with comorbid conditions or prescribe medication, school counselors, pastoral counselors, or other providers with unique specialties.

Mental health professionals who are flexible, collegial, and nonjudgmental are certain to find working with transgendered clients to be a fascinating and highly rewarding endeavor.

–Appendix A–
Standards of Care for Gender Identity Disorders

What follows is a brief reference guide to the *Standards of Care*. The complete text of the *Standards of Care* is available from the Harry Benjamin International Gender Dysphoria Association.

The Purpose of the Standards of Care. The major purpose of the *Standards of Care* is to articulate this international organization's professional consensus about the psychiatric, psychologic, medical, and surgical management of gender identity disorders. Professionals may use this document to understand the parameters within which they may offer assistance to those with these problems. Persons with gender identity disorders, their families, and social institutions may use the Standards of Care as a means to understand the current thinking of professionals. All readers should be aware of the limitations of knowledge in this area and of the hope that some of the clinical uncertainties will be resolved in the future through scientific investigation.

The Standards of Care are Clinical Guidelines. The *Standards of Care* are intended to provide flexible directions for the treatment of gender identity disorders. When eligibility requirements are stated they are meant to be minimum requirements. Individual professionals and organized programs may raise them. Clinical departures from these guidelines may come about because of a patient's unique anatomic, social, or psychological situation, an experienced professional's evolving method of handling a common situation, or a research protocol. These departures should be recognized as such, explained to the patient, documented both for legal protection and so that the short and long term results can be retrieved to help the field to evolve.

I. Professional involvement with patients with gender identity disorders involves any of the following:

   A. Diagnostic assessment
   B. Psychotherapy
   C. Real life experience
   D. Hormonal therapy
   E. Surgical therapy

II. **The Roles of the Mental Health Professional with the Gender Patient.**

   Mental health professionals who work with individuals with gender identity disorders may be regularly called upon to carry out many of these responsibilities:

   A. To accurately diagnose the individual's gender disorder according to either the *DSM-IV* or *ICD-10* nomenclature
   B. To accurately diagnose any co-morbid psychiatric conditions and see to their appropriate treatment
   C. To counsel the individual about the range of treatment options and their implications
   D. To engage in psychotherapy
   E. To ascertain eligibility and readiness for hormone and surgical therapy
   F. To make formal recommendations to medical and surgical colleagues
   G. To document their patient's relevant history in a letter of recommendation
   H. To be a colleague on a team of professionals with interest in the gender identity disorders
   I. To educate family members, employers, and institutions about gender identity disorders
   J To be available for follow-up of previously seen gender patients.

III. **The Training of Mental Health Professionals**
   A. The Adult-Specialist
      1. basic clinical competence in diagnosis and treatment of mental or emotional disorders

2. the basic clinical training may occur within any formally credentialing discipline—for example, psychology, psychiatry, social work, counseling, or nursing.
3. recommended minimal credentials for special competence with the gender identity disorders:
   a. master's degree or its equivalent in a clinical behavioral science field granted by an institution accredited by a recognized national or regional accrediting board
   b. specialized training and competence in the assessment of the *DSM-IV/ICD-10* Sexual Disorders (not simply gender identity disorders)
   c. documented supervised training and competence in psychotherapy
   d. continuing education in the treatment of gender identity disorders

B. The Child-Specialist
1. training in childhood and adolescent developmental psychopathology
2. competence in diagnosing and treating the ordinary problems of children and adolescents

IV. **The Differences between Eligibility and Readiness Criteria for Hormones or Surgery**
A. Eligibility—the specified criteria that must be documented before moving to a next step in a triadic therapeutic sequence (real life experience, hormones, and surgery)
B. Readiness—the specified criteria that rest upon the clinician's judgment prior to taking the next step in a triadic therapeutic sequence

V. **The Mental Health Professional's Documentation Letters for Hormones or Surgery Should Succinctly Specify:**
A. The patient's general identifying characteristics
B. The initial and evolving gender, sexual, and other psychiatric diagnoses

C. The duration of their professional relationship including the type of psychotherapy or evaluation that the patient underwent

D. The eligibility criteria that have been met and the mental health professional's rational for hormones or surgery

E. The patient's ability to follow the *Standards of Care* to date and the likelihood of future compliance

F. Whether the author of the report is part of a gender team or is working without benefit of an organized team approach

G. The offer of receiving a phone call to verify that the documentation letter is authentic

VI. **One Letter is Required for Instituting Hormone Treatment; Two Letters are Required for Surgery**

A. Two separate letters of recommendation from mental health professionals who work alone without colleagues experienced with gender identity disorders are required for surgery and

1. If the first letter is from a person with a master's degree, the second letter should be from a psychiatrist or a clinical psychologist—those who can be expected to adequately evaluate co-morbid psychiatric conditions.

2. If the first letter is from the patient's psychotherapist, the second letter should be from a person who has only played an evaluative role for the patient. Each letter writer, however, is expected to cover the same seven elements.

B. One letter with two signatures is acceptable if the mental health professionals conduct their tasks and periodically report on these processes to a team of other mental health professionals and non-psychiatric physicians.

VII. **Children with Gender Identity Disorders**

A. The initial task of the child-specialist mental health professional is to provide careful diagnostic assessments of gender-disturbed children.

1. the child's gender identity and gender role behaviors, family dynamics, past traumatic experiences, and general psychological health are separately assessed. Gender-disturbed children differ significantly along these parameters.
2. hormonal and surgical therapies should never be undertaken with this age group
3. treatment over time may involve family therapy, marital therapy, parent guidance, individual therapy of the child, or various combinations
4. treatment should be extended to all forms of psychopathology, not simply the gender disturbance.

VIII. **Treatment of Adolescents**
   A. In typical cases the treatment is conservative because gender identity development can rapidly and unexpectedly evolve. Teenagers should be followed, provided psychotherapeutic support, educated about gender options, and encouraged to pay attention to other aspects of their social, intellectual, vocational, and interpersonal development.
   B. They may be eligible for beginning triadic therapy as early as age 18, preferably with parental consent.
      1. Parental consent presumes a good working relationship between the mental health professional and the parents, so that they, too, fully understand the nature of the gender identity disorder.
      2. In many European counties sixteen to eighteen-year-olds are legal adults for medical decision making, and do not require parental consent. In the United States, age 18 is legal adulthood.
   C. Hormonal Therapy for Adolescents. Hormonal treatment should be conducted in two phases onlyafter puberty is well established.
      1. in the initial phase biological males should be administered an anti-androgen (which neutralizes testosterone effects only) or an LHRH agonist (which stops the production of testosterone only)

143

2. biological females should be administered sufficient androgens, progestins, or LHRH agonists (which stop the production of estradiol, estrone, and progesterone) to stop menstruation.
3. second phase treatments—after these changes have occurred and the adolescent's mental health remains stable
    a. biologic males may be given estrogenic agents
    b. biologic females may be given higher masculinizing doses of androgens
    c. second phase medications produce irreversible changes

D. Prior to Age 18. In selected cases, the real life experience can begin at age 16, with or without first phase hormones. The administration of hormones to adolescents younger than age 18 should rarely be done.
1. first phase therapies to delay the somatic changes of puberty are best carried out in specialized treatment centers under supervision of, or in consultation with, an endocrinologist, and preferably, a pediatric endocrinologist, who is part of an interdisciplinary team.
2. two goals justify this intervention
    a. to gain time to further explore the gender and the other developmental issues in psychotherapy
    b. to make passing easier if the adolescent continues to pursue gender change
3. in order to provide puberty delaying hormones to a person less than age 18, the following criteria must be met
    a. throughout childhood they have demonstrated an intense pattern of cross-gender identity and aversion to expected gender role behaviors
    b. gender discomfort has significantly increased with the onset of puberty
    c. social, intellectual, psychological, and interpersonal development are limited as a consequence of their gender identity disorder

    d. serious psychopathology, except as a consequence of the gender identity disorder, is absent

    e. the family consents and participates in the triadic therapy

E. Prior to Age 16

Second phase hormones, those which induce opposite sex characteristics should not be given prior to age 16 years.

F. Mental Health Professional Involvement is an Eligibility Requirement for Triadic Therapy During Adolescence.

    1. To be eligible for the implementation of the real life experience or hormone therapy, the mental health professional should be involved with the patient and family for a minimum of six months.

    2. To be eligible for the recommendation of genital reconstructive surgery or mastectomy, the mental health professional should be integrally involved with the adolescent and the family for at least eighteen months.

    3. School-aged adolescents with gender identity disorders often are so uncomfortable due to negative peer interactions and a felt incapacity to participate in the roles of their biologic sex that they refuse to attend school

        a. Mental health professionals should be prepared to work collaboratively with school personnel to find ways to continue the educational and social development of their patients.

IX. **Psychotherapy with Adults**

A. Many adults with gender identity disorder find comfortable, effective ways of identifying themselves without the triadic treatment sequence, with or without psychotherapy

B. Psychotherapy is not an absolute requirement for triadic therapy

    1. Individual programs vary to the extent that they perceive the need for psychotherapy

    2. When the mental health professional's initial assessment leads to a recommendation for psychotherapy, the clinician should specify the goals of treatment, estimate its frequency and duration

3. The *Standards of Care* committee is wary of insistence on some minimum number of psychotherapy sessions prior to the real life experience, hormones, or surgery but expects individual programs to set these

4. If psychotherapy is not done by members of a gender team, the psychotherapist should be informed that a letter describing the patient's therapy may be requested so the patient can move on to the next phase of rehabilitation

C. Psychotherapy often provides education about a range of options not previously seriously considered by the patient. Its goals are:

1. to be realistic about work and relationships

2. to define and alleviate the patient's conflicts that may have undermined a stable lifestyle and to attempt to create a long-term stable lifestyle

3. to find a comfortable way to live within a gender role and body

D. Even when the initial goals are attained, mental health professionals should discuss the likelihood that no educational, psychotherapeutic, medical, or surgical therapy can permanently eradicate all psychological vestiges of the person's original sex assignment

X. **The Real-Life Experience**

A. Since changing one's gender role has immediate profound personal and social consequences, the decision to do so should be preceded by an awareness of what these familial, vocational, interpersonal, educational, economic, and legal consequences are likely to be.

B. when clinicians assess the quality of a person's real-life experience in the new gender role, the following abilities are reviewed

1. to maintain full or part-time employment

2. to function as a student

3. to function in community-based volunteer activity

4. to undertake some combination of items 1-3

5. to acquire a new (legal) first or last name
6. to provide documentation that persons other than the therapist know that the patient functions in the new gender role

XI. **Eligibility and Readiness Criteria for Hormone Therapy for Adults**
   A. Three eligibility criteria exist:
      1. age 18 years
      2. demonstrable knowledge of what hormones medically can and cannot do and their social benefits and risks
      3. **Either** a documented real-life experience should be undertaken for at least three months prior to the administration of hormones
      Or
      4. a period of psychotherapy of a duration specified by the mental health professional after the initial evaluation (usually a minimum of three months) should be undertaken
      5. under no circumstances should a person be provided hormones who has fulfilled neither criteria #3 nor #4
   B. Three readiness criteria exist:
      1. the patient has had further consolidation of gender identity during the real-life experience or psychotherapy
      2. the patient has made some progress in mastering other identified problems leading to improving or continuing stable mental health
      3. hormones are likely to be taken in a responsible manner
   C. Hormones can be given for those who do not initially want surgery or a real-life experience. They must be appropriately diagnosed however, and meet the criteria stated above for hormone administration.

XII. **Requirements for Genital Reconstructive and Breast Surgery**
   A. Six eligibility criteria for various surgeries exist and equally apply to biological males and biological females
      1. legal age of majority in the patient's nation

147

2. 12 months of continuous hormonal therapy for those without a medical contraindication
3. 12 months of successful continuous full time real-life experience. Periods of returning to the original gender may indicate ambivalence about proceeding and should not be used to fulfill this criterion
4. while psychotherapy is not an absolute requirement for surgery for adults, regular sessions may be required by the mental health professional throughout the real life experience at a minimum frequency determined by the mental health professional
5. knowledge of the cost, required lengths of hospitalizations, likely complications, and post-surgical rehabilitation requirements of various surgical approaches
6. awareness of different competent surgeons

  B. Two readiness criteria exist:
1. demonstrable progress in consolidating the new gender identity
2. demonstrable progress in dealing with work,family, and interpersonal issues resulting in a significantly better or at least a stable state of mental health

XIII. **Surgery**
  A. Genital, Breast, and Other Surgery for the Male to Female Patient
1. Surgical procedures may include orchiectomy, penectomy, vaginoplasty, augmentation mammaplasty, and vocal cord surgery.
2. Vaginoplasty requires both skilled surgery and postoperative treatment. Three techniques are: penile skin inversion, pedicled rectosigmoid transplant, or free skin graft to line the neovagina
3. Augmentation mammaplasty may be performed prior to vaginoplasty if the physician prescribing hormones and the surgeon have documented that breast enlargement after undergoing hormonal treatment for two years is not sufficient for comfort in the social gender

role. Other surgeries that may be performed to assist feminization include: reduction thyroid chondroplasty, liposuction of the waist, rhinoplasty, facial bone reduction, face-lift, and blephoroplasty.

B. Genital and Breast Surgery for the Female to Male Patient

1. Surgical procedures may include mastectomy, hysterectomy, salpingo-oophrectomy, vaginectomy, metoidioplasty, scrotoplasty, urethroplasty, and phalloplasty.

2. Current operative techniques for phalloplasty are varied. The choice of techniques may be restricted by anatomical or surgical considerations. If the objectives of phalloplasty are a neophallus of good appearance, standing micturition, and/or coital ability, the patient should be clearly informed that there are both several separate stages of surgery and frequent technical difficulties which require additional operations.

3. Reduction mammaplasty may be necessary as an early procedure for some large breasted individuals to make the real-life experience feasible.

4. Liposuction may be necessary for final body contouring

C. Postsurgical Follow-up by Professionals

1. Long term postoperative follow-up is one of the factors associated with a good psychosocial outcome.

2. Follow-up is essential to the patient's subsequent anatomic and medical health and to the surgeon's knowledge about the benefits and limitations of surgery.

   a. Postoperative patients may incorrectly exclude themselves from follow-up with the physician prescribing hormones as well as their surgeonand mental health professional.

   b. These clinicians are best able to prevent, diagnose, and treat possible long term medical conditions that are unique to the hormonally and surgically treated.

   c. Surgeons who are operating on patients who are coming from long distances should include personal follow-up in their care plan.

    d. Continuing long term follow-up has to be afford-
       able and available in the patient's geographic
       region.
    e. Postoperative patients also have general health con-
       cerns and should undergo regular medical screening
       according to recommended guidelines.
3. The need for follow-up extends beyond the endocrinologist and surgeon, however, to the mental health
professional, who having spent a longer period of time
with the patient than any other professional, is in an
excellent position to assist in any postoperative adjustment difficulties.

–Appendix B–
Resources

The Harry Benjamin
International Gender Dysphoria
Association, Inc. (HBIGDA)
1300 South 2nd Street,
Suite 180
Minneapolis, MN 55454
612-624-8078

The Society for the Scientific
Study of Sex (Quad-S)
P.O. Box 208
Mount Vernon, IA 52314
319-895-8407

American Association of Sex
Educators, Counselors and
Therapists (AASECT)
P.O. Box 238
Mount Vernon, IA 52314-0238
319-895-8407

International Foundation for
Gender Education (IFGE)
P.O. Box 229
Waltham, MA 02254-0229
781-899-2212
http://www.ifge.org
IFGE is a non-profit organization that provides education and
resources for the transgendered
community and the general public. It publishes a magazine,

holds national conventions, and
supports research on medical,
legal, and social issues facing the
community. It also maintains a
large bookstore of gender-related
materials.

Spouses/Partners International
Conference for Education
(SPICE)
Contact Dr. Peggy Rudd
P.O. Box 5304
Katy, TX 77491-5394
http://www.spice@tri-ess.com
SPICE is an organization providing support for genetic females
in committed relationships with
heterosexual cross-dressers. They
hold an annual national conference.

FTM International
1360 Mission Street,
Suite 200
San Francisco, CA 94103
415-553-5987 voice mail; 510-
547-4785 fax
email: tstgmen@best.com
http://www.ftm-int.org
A non-profit organization that

provides information on female-to-male issues. This organization publishes a resource guide and a newsletter and sponsors national conferences. It also offers support groups and referrals.

The International Conference on Transgender Law and Employment Policy (ICTLEP)
P.O. Box Drawer 1010
Cooperstown, NY 13326
607-547-4118 voice
713-777-0909 fax
email: ICTLPhdq@AOL.com
A non-profit organization that provides legal education regarding legal rights and employment policies for transgendered persons. It holds an annual conference and publishes the proceedings. It is an invaluable resource for attorneys with transgendered clients.

Center for Assistance, Research and Information on Transsexuality and Gender Identity (CARTIG)
B.P. 17.22
75810 Paris Cedex 17
France
CARTIG is a non-profit organization that provides support and education. It publishes a magazine (in French).

The Gender Centre
25 Morgan Street
(P.O. Box 266)
Petersham NSW 2049 Australia
61-569-2366 voice
61-569-1176 fax
This organization provides counseling, support, referrals, and a residential program, as well as producing a magazine. It also assists with HIV/AIDS and drug and alcohol dependence.

Ingersoll Gender Center
1812 East Madison #106
Seattle, WA 98122-2843
206-329-6651
http://www.halcyon.com/ingersol/iiihome.html
A non-profit organization offering support groups and distributing a newsletter as well as other gender-related information.

The Intersex Society of North America (ISNA)
P.O. Box 31791
San Francisco, CA 94131
415-575-3885
voice 415-252-8202 fax
email: cchase@isna.org
ISNA is an organization founded and operated by intersexuals, those born with ambiguous genitalia or mixed sexual anatomy. It provides support, education, and advocacy for new approaches to

the management of intersex children.

The Society for the Second Self (Tri-Ess)
8880 Belaire B2
Suite 104
Houston, TX 77036
A support organization for heterosexual cross-dressers that has some thirty chapters throughout the United States.

T-Son
Personal support and resources, contact
Karen Gross
216-691-4357
email: KittenGR@aol.com
Organizational questions, contact
Mary Boenke
540-890-3957
email: MaryBoenke@aol.com
PFLAG's Special Outreach Network is a support group of transgendered persons, family, and friends. It provides a help line to comfort families striving to cope with issues of transition and lobbies for transgender inclusion in national and local legislation. The parent organization, PFLAG, has active affiliates in over 400 cities in the U.S. and many other countries.

Los Angeles Gender Center
1923½ Westwood Blvd,
Suite 2
Los Angeles, CA 90025
310-475-8880
Provides counseling, support groups and education.

The New Health Foundation
1214 Lake Street
Evanston, IL 60201
847-328-3433
This organization assists members of the transgendered community by subsidizing medical care, facilitating education, and advocating for transgender rights. It is founded and comprised largely of professionals.

National Foundation of Transsexualism
ATTN: Anthony Bernard
1307 St. Catherine Street
Montreal, Quebec H2L 2H4
Canada
514-526-5892 voice
514-526-1060 fax

The Outreach Institute
126 Western Avenue,
Suite 246
Augusta, ME 04330
A non-profit corporation that provides resources and publishes a journal.

San Francisco Gender Information
P.O. Box 423602
San Francisco, CA 94142-3602
Provides referrals and networking services.

The Gender Political Advocacy Coalition (GenderPac)
733 15th Street NW,
7th Floor
Washington, DC 20005
202-347-3024
This is a group of transgendered organizations and citizens dedicated to the pursuit of gender, affectional, and racial equality.

The National Youth Advocacy Coalition (NYAC)
1711 Connecticut Avenue, N.W.
Suite 206
Washington, D. C. 20009
202-319-7596 voice
202-319-7365 fax
email: nyac@nyacyouth.org
This organization is committed to improving the lives of gays, lesbians, bisexual, and transgendered youth.

Transgender Liberation Coalition Inc. (TLC)
P. O. Box 208
Kings Cross
NSW 2011 Australia
02-358-5664
This community-based advocacy group promotes the rights of people with transgender issues and is involved with HIV/AIDS and anti-violence projects.

SETA Trans Center
P.O. Box 135
00251 Helsinki, Finland
90-411-135 voice
90-411-137 fax
email: transtuki@seta.fi
Finland's national association for transsexuals, cross-dressers, and sexual minorities. It offers support, networking, and education; pursues civil rights work; and produces a magazine.

Gender Programs

California:
Gender Dysphoria Program, Inc.
1515 El Camino Real
Palo, Alto, CA 94306
650-326-4645

Gender Dysphoria Program of
Orange County
32158 Camino Capistrano, Suite
203
San Juan Capistrano, CA 92675
714-240-7020

Colorado:
Institute for Gender Study and
Treatment
P.O. Box 126
Arvada, CO 80001
303-420-9885

Connecticut:
Gender Identity Clinic of New
England
68 Adelaide Road
Manchester, CT 06040
860-646-8651

Florida:
Gender Identity Association
6144 Gazebo Park Place, So.
Suite # 102
Jacksonville, FL 32257
902-260-3400

Michigan:
University of Michigan Medical
Center Comprehensive Gender
Services Program
1500 E. Medical Center Drive
UH 1H223
Ann Arbor, MI 48109-0050
313-936-7067

Minnesota:
University of Minnesota
Program in Human Sexuality
Transgender Services
1300 South 2nd Street,
Suite 180
Minneapolis, MN 55454-1015
612-625-1500

Ohio:
Central Ohio Gender Dysphoria
Program
P.O. Box 82008
Columbus, OH 43202
614-451-0111

Texas:
Rosenberg Clinic, Gender
Treatment Program
1103 Rosenberg Avenue
Galveston, TX 77550
409-763-0016

Virginia:
Horton Gender Program
Hague Medical Center
330 W. Brambleton Avenue,
Suite 230
Norfolk, VA 23510
804-622-7500

Wisconsin:
Milwaukee Transgender
Program, Pathways Counseling
Center
2645 N. Mayfair Road, Suite
230, First Financial Building
Milwaukee, WI 53226-1304
414-774-4111

Canada:
Vancouver Hospital Centre for
Sexuality, Gender Identity and
Reproductive Health
855 West 12th Avenue
Vancouver, B.C. V5Z 1M9
Canada
604-875-8282

Gender Identity Clinic: Clarke
Institute of Psychiatry
250 College Street
Toronto, Ontario M5T 1R8
Canada
416-979-2221

The Netherlands:
Gender Team Amsterdam
Free University Hospital
P. O. Box 7057
1007 MB Amsterdam, The
Netherlands
31-20-444-4444

United Kingdom:
The Charing Cross Gender
Clinic: Gender Identity Program
Charing Cross Hospital
Fulham Palace Road
London, W6 8RF, UK
44-81-846-1516

–Appendix C–
A Cross-Gender Questionnaire

Richard E. Docter & James S. Fleming

Please respond to each item by agreeing (yes) or disagreeing (no). Please respond to all 55 items.

1. When I wear women's clothing I do not consider it "crossdressing" because my true gender is feminine (or mostly feminine).
2. I have an alternative "fantasy" cross-dressing wardrobe which is too sexy to wear in public.
3. I have adopted a feminine name which is now my legalname.
4. If I am wearing a sexy dress, I sometimes feel more attracted to men.
5. I believe I am a "woman in a man's body."
6. Sometimes I have acquired more sets of fancy underwear or other sexy clothing than I need.
7. I have a driver's license or other valid identification showing my "female" picture and name.
8. I eat in restaurants in my feminine role several times a year.
9. In my feminine role, I usually feel like I am a woman.
10. Sometimes I get a sexual thrill when I see my feminine image in a mirror.
11. While in the feminine role men I did not know have bought me refreshments or drinks.
12. I have lived entirely (or almost entirely) as a woman for more than six consecutive months.
13. I prefer to think of my feminine name as my real name.
14. While in the feminine role, I have been escorted to a restaurant by a man as his date.
15. When I feel tense, wearing something feminine will usually make me feel a little more calm.
16. I have lived entirely (or almost entirely) as a woman for one year or longer.

17. I can experience feelings of being female at any time, no matter how I am dressed.
18. Buying and using beautiful makeup will often make me feel sexually excited.
19. I have received ten or more hours of electrolysis.
20. I have received fifty or more hours of electrolysis.
21. While in the feminine role, I have been escorted to some kind of event by a man on a date.
22. Even when not in the feminine role I reveal some feminine mannerisms (or I used to).
23. Putting on lipstick or perfume often makes me feel erotic or sexy.
24. I can enjoy being a woman, but at other times I enjoy functioning like a man.
25. I often prefer hosiery and high heels to the more ordinary style many women wear.
26. Being in the feminine role is almost always a sexually arousing experience for me.
27. While in the feminine role, I have danced with a man.
28. Wearing beautiful lingerie usually gives me some sexual excitement.
29. When in my feminine role I feel I am expressing my "true self," not putting on an act.
30. I have talked to a physician about obtaining female hormones (whether obtained them or not).
31. While in the feminine role, I have been passionately kissed on the lips by a man.
32. If it were possible, I'd choose to live my life as a woman (or I do so now).
33. Some specific articles of clothing usually have an especially powerful effect on my sexual arousal.
34. I have taken female hormones regularly for three months or longer.
35. While in the feminine role, I have had a physical encounter with a man that went beyond kissing.
36. When I must put aside my feminine role for even a short time, it is very hard for me to do so.
37. Wearing beautiful clothes and makeup often brings me greater sexual pleasure than other sexual activities.
38. Often I become sexually excited just thinking about being a woman.
39. I have taken female hormones regularly for six months or longer.

40. As a man, I am exclusively attracted to women.
41. I almost always wear one or more items of feminine apparel under my male clothes.
42. I often become sexually excited when I shop for women's clothing, shoes, or makeup.
43. I have taken female hormones regularly for a year or longer.
44. As a man, I am attracted to both women and men (not necessarily equally).
45. I daydream or think about being a woman at least once a day.
46. I often become sexually excited when I read about men who become women.
47. I have discussed with a physician possible (or actual) cosmetic surgery to improve my feminine appearance.
48. In the feminine role, I am exclusively attracted to women.
49. I daydream or think about being a woman at least ten times each day.
50. Being in the feminine role is a super-pleasure for me.
51. I have received a small amount (or more) of cosmetic surgery to improve my feminine appearance.
52. When in the feminine role, I am attracted to both men and women (not necessarily equally).
53. After several hours (or days) in the feminine role I'm usually ready to change back into men's clothes.
54. Being in the feminine role often produces strong feelings of exhilaration.
55. On one (or more) occasions, while in the feminine role I have had a sexual encounter with a man.

Scoring

1. Here are the "yes" and the "no" items for the Cross-Gender Identity Scale. Count the total number of the following items (1, 5, 9, 13, 17, 22, 29, 32, 36, 41, 45, 49) you marked as "yes". Then total the items 24 or 53 you marked as "no."
   Add your total "yes" items and "no" items for this scale
   IDENTITY TOTAL =

2. Here are the "yes" and the "no" items for the Feminization Scale. Count the total number of the following items (3, 7, 8, 12, 16, 19,

20, 30, 34, 39, 43, 47, 51) you marked as "yes." This scale does
not use any "no" items.
Add your total items for this scale.
FEMINIZATION TOTAL =

3. Here are the "yes" and the "no" items for the Sexual Arousal
    Scale. Count the total number of the following items (2,6, 10, 15,
    18, 23, 25, 26, 28, 33, 37, 38, 42, 46, 50, 54) you marked as
    "yes," This scale does not use any "no" items.
    Add your total items for this scale.
    AROUSAL TOTAL =

4. Here are the "yes" and the "no" items for the Cross-Gender Role
    Scale. Count the total number of the following items (4, 11, 14,
    21, 27, 31, 35, 44, 52, 55) you marked as "yes." Then total the
    items 40 or 48 which you marked as "no."
    Add your total "yes" and "no" items for this scale.
    GENDER ROLE TOTAL =

Results

Comparison Results for	Transvestites	Transsexuals
Identity	7	12
Feminization	2	10
Arousal	9	4
Gender Role	4	8

Compare your totals to these average totals to get an indication of
where you fall on the continuum.

References

Abramowitz, S. (1986). Psychological outcomes of sex reassignment surgery. *Journal of Consulting and Clinical Psychology, 54*, 183–189.

American Psychiatric Association. (1994). *Diagnostic and statistical manual of mental disorders* (4th ed.). Washington, DC: Author.

Asscheman, H., Gooren, L., & Assies, J. (1988). Prolactin levels and pituitary enlargement in hormone-treated male-to-female transsexuals. *Clinical Endocrinology, 28*, 583–588.

Auge, R. , Fraser, L., Henkin, W., Hraca, K., Rodgers, L., & Vitale, A. (1997). *A transgender issues consultation group in the San Francisco Bay area.* Paper presented at the fifteenth international symposium on gender dysphoria, Harry Benjamin International Gender Dysphoria Association, Vancouver, Canada.

Bakker, A., van Kesteren, P. J., Gooren, L. J., & Bezemer, P. D. (1993). The prevalence of transsexualism in The Netherlands. *Acta Psychiatrica Scandinavica, 87*(4), 237–238.

Balen, A. H., Schachter, M. E., Montgomery, D., Reid, R. W., & Jacobs, H. S. Polycystic ovaries are a common finding in untreated female to male transsexuals. *Clinical Endocrinology, 38*(3), 325–329.

Barbier, P. (1996). *The world of the castrati: The history of an extraordinary operatic phenomenon.* London: Souvenir Press.

Barlow, D. H., Abel, G. G., & Blanchard, E. B. (1977). Gender identity change in a transsexual: An exorcism. *Archives of Sexual Behavior, 6* (5), 387–395.

Barrett, J. (1998). Psychological and social function before and after phalloplasty. [on-line]. *International Journal of Transgenderism, 2*(1). Abstract.

Becking, A. G., Tuinzing, D. B., Hage, J. J., & Gooren, L.J. (1996). Facial corrections in male to female transsexuals: A preliminary report on 16 patients. *Journal of Oral and Maxillofacial Surgery, 54*(4), 413–419.

Belli, M. (1978). Transsexual surgery: A new tort? *Journal of the American Medical Association, 239*(20), 2143–2148.

Benjamin, H. (1953). Transvestism and transsexualism. *International Journal of Sexology, 7*, 12–14.

Benjamin, H. (1954). Transsexualism and transvestism as psychosomatic and somato-psychic syndromes: symposium. *American Journal of Psychotherapy, 8*, 219–230.

Benjamin, H. (1964). Clinical aspects of transsexualism in male and female. *American Journal of Psychotherapy, 18*, 458–469.

Benjamin, H. (1964). Nature and management of transsexualism with a report on 31 operated cases. *Western Journal of Surgery: Obstetrics and Gynecology, 72,* 105–111.

Benjamin, H. (1966). *The transsexual phenomenon.* New York: Julian Press.

Benjamin, H. (1967). Transvestism and transsexualism in the male and female. *Journal of Sex Research, 3,* 107–127.

Benjamin, H. (1969). For the practicing physician: Suggestions and guidelines for the management of transsexuals. In R. Green & J. Money (Eds.), *Transsexualism and sex reassignment* (pp. 305–307). Baltimore: Johns Hopkins University Press.

Benjamin, H. (1971). Should surgery be performed on transsexuals? *American Journal of Psychotherapy, 25,* 74–82.

Benjamin, H., & Ihlenfeld, C. L. (1973). Transsexualism. *American Journal of Nursing, 73,* 457–461.

Bentler, P. M., & Prince, C. (1970). Psychiatric symptomatology in transvestites. *Journal of Clinical Psychology, 26,* 434–435.

Blanchard, R. (1985) Typology of male-to-female transsexualism. *Archives of Sexual Behavior, 14,* 247–261.

Blanchard, R. (1988). Nonhomosexual gender dysphoria. *Journal of Sex Research, 24,* 188–193.

Blanchard, R. (1989). The classification and labeling of nonhomosexual gender dysphorias. *Archives of Sexual Behavior, 18,* 315–334.

Blanchard, R. (1989). The concept of autogynephilia and the typology of male gender dysphoria. *Journal of Nervous and Mental Disorders, 177,* 616–623.

Blanchard, R. (1990). Gender identity disorders in adult men. In R. Blanchard and B. W. Steiner (Eds.) *Clinical management of gender identity disorders in children and adults* (pp. 77–91). Washington, DC: American Psychiatric Press.

Blanchard, R. (1994). A structural equation model for age at clinical presentation in nonhomosexual male gender dysphorics. *Archives of Sexual Behavior, 23*(3), 311–320.

Blanchard, R., Steiner, B. W., & Clemmenson, L., (1985). Gender dysphoria, gender reorientation, and the clinical management of transsexualism. *Journal of Consulting and Clinical Psychology, 53,* 295–304.

Blanchard, R., Steiner, B. W., Clemmensen, L. H., & Dickey, R. (1989). Prediction of regrets in postoperative transsexuals. *Canadian Journal of Psychiatry, 34*(1), 43–45.

Bockting, W. O., & Coleman, E. (1992). A comprehensive approach to a treatment of gender dysphoria. In W. O. Bockting & E. Coleman (Eds.), *Gender dysphoria: Interdisciplinary approaches in clinical management* (pp. 131–155). New York: Haworth.

Bodlund, O., Kullgren, G., Sundbom, E., & Hojerback, T. (1993). Personality traits and disorders among transsexuals. *Acta Psychiatrica Scandinavica, 88*(5), 322–327.

References

Bosinski, H. A., Peter, M., Bonatz, G., Arndt, R., Heidenreich,M., Sippell, W. G., & Wille, R. (1997a). A higher rate of hyperandrogenic disorders in female-to-male transsexuals. *Psychoneuroendocrinology, 22*(5), 361–380.

Boskinski, H. A., Schroder, I., Peter, M., Arndt, R., Wille, R., & Sippell, W. G. (1997b). Anthropometrical measurements and androgen levels in males, females, and hormonally untreated female-to-male transsexuals. *Archives of Sexual Behavior, 26*(2), 143–157.

Botzer, M. C., Vehrs, B., & Biber, S. (1993). *Factors contributing to favorable outcomes of gender reassignment surgery.* Paper presented at the thirteenth international symposium on gender dysphoria, Harry Benjamin International Gender Dysphoria Association, New York.

Bradley, S. J. (1980). Female transsexualism: a child and adolescent perspective. *Child Psychiatry and Human Development, 11*(1), 12–18.

Brooks, G., & Brown, G. R. (1994). *International survey of 851 transgendered men: the Boulton and Park experience.* Paper presented at the sixth annual Texas "T" party. San Antonio, Texas.

Brown, G. R. (1988). Transsexuals in the military: Flight into hypermasculinity. *Archives of Sexual Behavior, 17*(6), 527–537.

Brown, G. R. (1990a). A review of clinical approaches to gender dysphoria. *Journal of Clinical Psychiatry, 51,* 57–64.

Brown, G. R. (1990b). The transvestite husband. *Medical Aspects of Human Sexuality, 24,* 35–42.

Brown, G. R. (1994). 106 women in relationships with cross-dressing men: A descriptive study from a nonclinical population. *Archives of Sexual Behavior, 23,* 515–529.

Brown, G. R. (1995). Transvestism. In G. O. Gabbard (Ed.), *Treatments of psychiatric disorders* (2nd ed.). Washington, DC: American Psychiatric Press.

Brown, G. R., Wise, T. N., Costa, P. T., Herbst, J. H., Fagan, P. J., & Schmidt, C. W. (1996). Personality characteristics and sexual functioning of 188 cross-dressing men. *Journal of Nervous and Mental Disease, 184*(5), 265–273.

Buhrich, N. (1978). Motivation for cross-dressing in heterosexual transvestism. *Acta Psychiatrica Scandinavica, 57*(2), 145–152.

Buhrich, N., Barr, R., & Lam-Po-Tang, P. R. (1978). Two transsexuals with 47-XYY karyotype. *British Journal of Psychiatry, 133,* 77–81.

Buhrich, N., & McConaghy, N. (1977). The discrete syndromes of transvestism and transsexualism. *Archives of Sexual Behavior, 6*(6), 483–495.

Buhrich, N. & McConaghy, N. (1978). Parental relationships during childhood in homosexuality, transvestism, and transsexualism. *Australian and New Zealand Journal of Psychiatry, 12*(2), 103–108.

Burke, P. (1996). *Gender shock.* New York: Doubleday.

Clare, D., & Tully, B. (1989). Transhomosexuality, or the dissociation of sexual orientation and sex object choice. *Archives of Sexual Behavior, 18*(6), 531–536.

Cohen, L., de Ruiter, C., Ringelberg, H., & Cohen-Kettenis, P. T. (1997). Psychological functioning of adolescent transsexuals: Personality and psychopathology. *Journal of Clinical Psychology, 53*(2), 187–196.

Cohen-Kettenis, P. T., & van Goozen, S. H. M. (1997). Sex reassignment of adolescent transsexual: A follow-up study. *Journal of the American Academy of child and Adolescent Psychiatry, 36*(2), 263–271.

Cole, C. M., O'Boyle, M., Emory, L. E., & Meyer W. J. (1997). Comorbidity of gender dysphoria and other major psychiatric diagnoses. *Archives of Sexual Behavior, 26*(1), 13–26.

Coleman, E., & Bockting, W. O. (1988). "Heterosexual" prior to sex reassignment—"Homosexual" afterwards: a case study of a female-to-male transsexual. *Journal of Psychology and Human Sexuality, 1*(2), 69–82.

Coleman, E., Bockting, W. O., & Gooren, L. (1993). Homosexual and bisexual identity in sex-reassigned female-to-male transsexuals. *Archives of Sexual Behavior, 22*(1), 37–50.

Coleman, E., & Cesnik, J., (1990). Skoptic syndrome: the treatment of an obsessional gender dysphoria with lithium carbonate and psychotherapy. *American Journal of Psychotherapy, 44*(2), 204–217.

Coleman, E., Colgan, P., & Gooren, L. (1992). Male cross-gender behavior in Myanmar (Burma): a description of the acault. *Archives of Sexual Behavior, 21*(3), 313–321.

Corsini, R. J. (Ed.) . (1977) . *Current personality theories.* Itasca, IL: F. E. Peacock.

Costa-Santos, J., & Madeira, R. (1996). Transsexualism in Portugal: The legal framework and procedure, and its consequences for transsexuals. *Medicine, Science and the Law, 36*(3), 221–225.

Crews, D. (1994, November). Animal sexuality. *Scientific American,* 108–114.

Crovitz, E. (1976). Treatment of the transsexual and medicolegal issues. *Forensic Science, 7*(1), 1–8.

Davenport, C. W. (1986). A follow-up study of ten feminine boys. *Archives of Sexual Behavior, 15*(6), 511–517.

De Cuypere, G., Janes, C., & Rubens, R., (1995). Psychosocial functioning of transsexuals in Belgium. *Acta Psychiatrica Scandinavica, 91*(3), 180–184.

Diamond, M., & Sigmundson, K., (1997). *Case study presentation.* Presented at the fifteenth international symposium on gender dysphoria, Harry Benjamin International Gender Dysphoria Association, Vancouver, Canada.

Devor, H. (1993). Sexual orientation identities, attractions, and practices of female-to-male transsexuals. *Journal of Sex Research, 30,* 303–315.

Di Ceglie, D., Sturge, C., & Sutton, A. (1998). Gender identity disorders in children and adolescents guidance for management [on-line]. *International Journal of Transgenderism, 2*(2).

Dickey, R., & Stephens, J. (1995). Female-to-male transsexualism, heterosexual type: Two cases. *Archives of Sexual Behavior, 24*(4), 439–445.

Docter, R. (1988). *Toward a theory of cross-gender behavior.* New York: Plenum.

Docter, R., & Fleming, J. S., (1992). Dimensions of transvestism and transsexualism: The validation and factorial structure of the cross-gender questionnaire. In W. O. Bockting & E. Coleman (Eds.), *Gender dysphoria: Interdisciplinary approaches in clinical management* (pp. 15–37). New York: Haworth.

Dorner, G., Poppe, I., Stahl, F., Kolzsch, J., & Uebelhack, R. (1991). Gene and environment-dependent neuroendocrine etiogenesis of homosexuality and transsexualism. *Experimental and Clinical Endocrinology, 98*(2), 141–150.

Dynes, W. R. (Ed.),(1990). *Encyclopedia of homosexuality.* New York: Garland.

Edgerton, M. T. (1984). The role of surgery in the treatment of transsexualism. *Annals of Plastic Surgery, 13*(6), 473–481.

Edgerton, M. T., Knorr, N. J., & Callison, J. R. (1969). *The surgical treatment of transsexual patients: Limitations and indications.* Paper presented at the annual meeting of the American Association of Plastic Surgeons, San Francisco.

Edgerton, M. T., & Meyer, J. (1973). Surgical and psychiatric aspects of transsexualism. In C. Horton (Ed.) *Plastic and reconstructive surgery of the genital area.* Boston: Little, Brown.

Ehrhardt, A. A., Grisanti, G., & McCauley, E. A. (1979). Female-to-male transsexuals compared to lesbians: behavioral patterns of childhood and adolescent development. *Archives of Sexual Behavior, 8*(6), 481–490.

Eicher, W., Spoljar, M., Murken, J. D., Richter, K., Cleve, H., & Stengel-Rutkowski, S. (1981). [Transsexualism and the H-Y antigen] , (abstract), *Fortschritte Der Medizin, 99*(1–2), 9–12.

Eicher, W., Spoljar, M., Richter, K., Cleve, H., Murker, J. D., Stengel-Rutkowki, S., & Steindl, E. (1980). [Transsexuality and X-Y antigen], (abstract), *Geburtshilfe und Frauenheilkunde, 40*(6), 529–540.

Eldh, J., Berg, A., & Gustagsson, M. (1997). Long-term follow up after sex reassignment surgery. Scandinavian *Journal of Plastic and Reconstructive Surgery and Hand Surgery, 31*(1), 39–45.

Elias, A. N., & Valenta, L. J. (1992). Are all males equal? Anatomic and functional basis for sexual orientation in males. *Medical Hypotheses, 39*(1), 85–87.

Ellis, H. (1936a). *Studies in the psychology of sex.* New York: Random House.

Ellis, H. (1936b). *Studies in the psychology of sex: Eonism and other supplementary studies, 7.* New York: Random House.

Emory, L. E., Williams, D. H., Cole, C. M., Amparo, E. G., Meyer, W. J. (1991). Anatomic variation of the corpus callosum in persons with gender dysphoria. *Archives of Sexual Behavior, 20*(4), 409–417.

Engel, W., Pfafflin, F., & Wiedeking, C. (1980). H-Y antigen in transsexuality, and how to explain testis differentiation in H-Y antigen-negative males and ovary differentiation in H-Y antigen positive females. *Human Genetics, 55*(3), 315–319.

Ettner, R. (1995). *Workshop model for the inclusion of the families of transsexuals.* Poster session presented at the fourteenth international symposium on gender dysphoria, Harry Benjamin International Gender Dysphoria Association, Bavaria, Germany.

Ettner, R. (1996). *Confessions of a gender defender.* Evanston, IL: Chicago Spectrum Press.

Ettner, R., Schacht, M., Brown, J., Niederberger, C., & Schrang, E. (1996). *Transsexualism: The phenotypic variable.* Poster session presented at the fifteenth international symposium on gender dysphoria, Harry Benjamin International Gender Dysphoria Association, Vancouver, Canada.

Eyler, A. & Wright, K. (1995).*Gender identification and sexual orientation among genetic females with gender-blended self-perception in childhood and adolescence.* Paper presented at the fourteenth international symposium on gender dysphoria, Harry Benjamin International Gender Dysphoria Association, Germany.

Feinberg, L. (1996). *Transgender warriors.* Boston: Beacon Press.

Fleming, M., Cohen, D., Salt, P., Jones, D. & Jenkins, S. (1981). A study of pre-and postsurgical transsexuals: MMPI characteristics. *Archives of Sexual Behavior, 10*(2), 161–170.

Fleming, M., MacGowan, B., & Costos, D. (1985). The dyadic adjustment of female-to-male transsexuals. *Archives of Sexual Behavior, 14*(1), 47–55.

Fleming, M., Steinman, C., & Bocknek, G. (1980). Methodological problems in assessing sex-reassignment surgery: a reply to Meyer and Reter. *Archives of Sexual Behavior, 9,* 451–456.

Freund, K., Steiner, B. W., & Chan, S. (1982). Two types of cross-gender identity. *Archives of Sexual Behavior, 11*(1), 49–63.

Futterweit, W., (1980). Endocrine management of transsexuals: hormonal profiles of serum prolactin, testosterone, and estradiol. New York *State Journal of Medicine, 80,* 1261–1264.

Futterweit, W. (1983). Pituitary tumors and polycystic ovarian disease. *Obstetrics and Gynecology, 62,* S78–S79.

Futterweit, W. (1998). Endocrine therapy of transsexualism and potential complications of long-term treatment. *Archives of Sexual Behavior, 27*(2), 209–225.

Futterweit, W. & Deligdisch, L. (1986). Histopathological effects of exogenously administered testosterone in nineteen female-to-male transsexuals. *Journal of Clinical Endocrinology and Metabolism, 62,* 16–21.

References

Futterweit, W., & Krieger, D. T. (1979). Pituitary tumors associated with hyper prolactinemia and polycystic ovarian disease. *Fertility and Sterility, 31,* 608–613.

Futterweit, W., Weiss, R. A., & Fagerstrom, R. M. (1986). Endocrine evaluation of forty female-to-male transsexuals: increased frequency of polycystic ovarian disease in female transsexualism. *Archives of Sexual Behavior, 15,* 69–78.

Gallarda, T., Amado, I., Coussinoux, S., Poirier, M. F., Cordier, B., & Olie, J. P. (1997). [The transsexualism syndrome: clinical aspects and therapeutic prospects]. *Encephale, 23*(5), 321–326.

Garber, M. (1993). *Vested interests: Cross-dressing and cultural anxiety.* New York: HarperCollins.

Gilbert, D. A. Winslow, B. H., Gilbert, D. M., Jordan, G. H., & Horton, C. E. (1988). Transsexual surgery in the genetic female. *Clinics in Plastic Surgery, 15*(3), 471–487.

Gilpin, D. C., Raza, S., & Gilpin, D. (1979). Transsexual symptoms in a male child treated by a female therapist. *American Journal of Psychotherapy, 3*(3), 453–463.

Giordano, G., & Giusti, M. (1995). Hormones and psychosexual differentiation. *Minerva Endocrinologica, 20*(3), 165–193.

Godlewski, J. (1988). Transsexualism and anatomic sex ratio reversal in Poland. *Archives of Sexual Behavior, 17*(6), 547–548.

Gooren, L. (1986). The neuroendocrine response of luteinizing hormone to estrogen administration in heterosexual, homosexual, and transsexual subjects. *Journal of Clinical Endocrinology and Metabolism, 63*(3), 583–588.

Gooren, L. (1990). The endocrinology of transsexualism: a review and commentary. *Psychoneuroendocrinology, 15*(1), 3–14.

Gottlieb, L. J., & Levine, A. L. (1993). A new design for the radial forearm free-flap phallic construction. *Plastic and Reconstructive Surgery, 92,* 276–283.

Grasser, T., Keidel, M., & Kockott, G. (1989). [Frequency analytic EEG study on the topic of temporal function disorders in transsexuality], (abstract). *EEG EMG, 20,* (2), 117–120.

Green, R. (1974). *Sexual identity conflict in children and adults.* New York: Basic Books.

Green, R. (1975). Sexual identity: Research strategies. *Archives of Sexual Behavior, 5,* 425–446.

Green, R. (1979). Childhood cross-gender behavior and subsequent sexual preference. *American Journal of Psychiatry, 136,* 106–108.

Green, R. (1985). Gender identity in childhood and later sexual orientation: follow up of 78 males. *American Journal of Psychiatry, 142,* 339–341.

Green, R. (1987). *The sissy boy syndrome and the development of homosexuality.* New Haven, CT: Yale University Press.

Green, R. (1993). *Transsexualism and the law.* Paper presented at the thirteenth international symposium on gender dysphoria, Harry Benjamin International Gender Dysphoria Association, New York.

Green, R., & Money, J. (Eds.). (1969). *Transsexualism and Sex Reassignment.* Baltimore: Johns Hopkins University Press.

Greenberg, R. P., & Laurence, L. (1981). A comparison of the MMPI results for psychiatric patients and male applicants for transsexual surgery. *Journal of Nervous and Mental Disease, 169*(5), 320–323.

Haber, C. H. (1991). The psychoanalytic treatment of a preschool boy with a gender identity disorder. *Journal of the American Psychoanalytic Association, 39*(1), 107–129.

Hage, J. J., & Bloem, J. J. (1993). Review of the literature on construction of a neourethra in female-to-male transsexuals. *Annals of Plastic Surgery, 30*(3), 278–286.

Hage, J. J., Bout, C.A., Bloem, J. J., & Megens, J. A. (1993). Phalloplasty in female-to-male transsexuals: What do our patients ask for? *Annals of Plastic Surgery, 30*(4), 323–326.

Hirschfield, M. (1910). *Die Transvestiten* [Transvestites]. Berlin: Pulvermacher.

Hoenig, J., & Kenna, J. C. (1979). EEG abnormalities and transsexualism. *British Journal of Psychiatry, 134,* 293–300.

Hoffman, M. (1969). Transsexualism. [Letter to the editor]. American Journal of Psychiatry, 126 (2), 155.

Jaffrey, Z. (1996). *The invisibles: A tale of the eunuchs of India.* New York: Pantheon.

Jarrar, K., Wolff, E., & Weidner, W. (1996). [Long-term outcome of sex reassignment of male transsexuals patients]. *Urologe, 35,*(4), 331–337.

Jorgensen, C. (1988). Personal communication in memorial for Harry Benjamin. *Archives of Sexual Behavior, 17*(1) 2–31.

Kavanaugh, J. G., Jr., & Volkan, V. D. (1978). Transsexualism and a new type of psychosurgery. *International Journal of Psychoanaltyic Psychotherapy, 7,* 366–372.

Kockott, G., & Fahrner, E. M. (1988). Male-to-female and female-to-male transsexuals: A comparison. *Archives of Sexual Behavior, 17*(6), 539–546.

Krafft-Ebing, R. von. (1886). *Psychopathia sexualis.* New York: G.P. Putnam's Sons, 1996.

Kuiper, B., & Cohen-Kettenis, P. (1988). Sex reassignment surgery: a study of 141 Dutch transsexuals. *Archives of Sexual Behavior, 17*(5), 439–457.

Kuiper, B., & Cohen-Kettenis, P. (1995). *Factors influencing post-operative "regret" in transsexuals.* Paper presented at the fourteenth international symposium on gender dysphoria, Harry Benjamin International Gender Dysphoria Association, Germany.

References

Kula, K., Dulko, S., Pawlikowski, M., Imielinski, K., & Slowikowska, J. (1986). A nonspecific disturbance of the gonadostat in women with transsexualism and isolated hypergonadotropism in the male-to-female disturbance of gender identity. *Experimental and Clinical Endocrinology, 87*(1), 8–14.

Lampe, L., & Szokoly, V. (1997). [Surgical management of masculine transsexualism]. *Orvosi-Hetilap, 138*(17), 1073–1078.

Landen, M., Walinder, J., & Lundstrom, B. (1996). Incidence and sex ratio of transsexualism in Sweden. *Acta Psychiatrica Scandinavica, 93*(4), 261–263.

Laub, D. R., & Fisk, N. (1974). A rehabilitation program for gender dysphoria syndrome by surgical sex change. *Plastic and Reconstructive Surgery, 53,* 388–403.

Lazer, S. , Benet, A. E., Rehman, J., Schaefer, L. C., & Melman, A. (1995). *The reported sex and surgery satisfactions of twenty-eight operated male-to-female transsexual patients.* Unpublished.

Leavitt, F., Berger, J. C., Hoeppner, J. A., & Northrop, G. (1980). Presurgical adjustment in male transsexuals with and without hormonal treatment. Journal of Nervous and Mental Disease, 168 (11), 693–697.

Levine, S. B. (1980). Psychiatric diagnosis of patients requesting sex reassignment surgery. *Journal of Sex and Marital Therapy, 6*(3), 164–173.

Levine, S. B. (1993). Gender-disturbed males. *Journal of Sex and Marital Therapy, 19*(2), 131–141.

Lief, H. I., & Hubschman, L. (1993). Orgasm in the postoperative transsexual. *Archives of Sexual Behavior, 22*(2), 145–155.

Loeb, L. (1992). Analysis of the transference neurosis in a child with transsexual symptoms. *Journal of the American Psychoanalytic Association, 40*(2), 587–605.

Loeb, L., & Shane, M. (1982). The resolution of a transsexual wish in a five-year-old boy. *Journal of the American Psychoanalytic Association, 30*(2), 419–434.

Lothstein, L. M. (1979). Psychodynamics and sociodynamics of gender-dysphoric states. *American Journal of Psychotherapy, 33*(2), 214–238.

Lothstein, L. M., (1984). Psychological testing with transsexuals: A 30-year review. *Journal of Personality Assessment, 48*(5), 500–507.

Lothstein, L. M., & Levine, S. B. (1981). Expressive psychotherapy with gender dysphoric patients. *Archives of General Psychiatry, 38*(8), 924–929.

Lundberg, P.O., Sjovall, A., & Walinder, J. (1975). Sella turcica in male-to-female transsexuals. *Archives of Sexual Behavior, 4*(6), 657–662.

Macvicar, K. (1978). The transsexual wish in a psychotic character. *International Journal of Psychoanaltyic Psychotherapy, 7,* 354–365.

Manipulating gender identity. (1998, July 7). *Chicago Sun-Times.* p.20.

Mate-Kole, C., Freschi, M., & Robin, A. (1990). A controlled study of psychological and social change after surgical gender reassignment in selected male transsexuals. *British Journal of Psychiatry, 157,* 261–264.

Mendelsohn, R. S. (1970, February). Surgical sex reassignment: A passionate judgment. *Medical World News, 50E.*

Meyer, J. K. (1982). The theory of gender identity disorders. *Journal of the American Psychoanalytic Association, 30*(2), 381–418.

Meyer, J. & Reter, D. (1979). Sex reassignment: follow-up. *Archives of General Psychiatry, 36,* 1010–1015.

Meyer-Bahlburg, H. F. (1982). Hormones and psychosexual differentiation; implications for the management of intersexuality, homosexuality and transsexuality. *Clinics in Endocrinology and Metabolism, 11*(3), 681–701.

Meyer-Bahlburg, H. F. (1994). Intersexuality and the diagnosis of gender identity disorder. *Archives of Sexual Behavior, 23,* 21–40.

Meyerowitz, J. (1998). Sex change and the popular press: Historical notes on transsexuality in the United States, 1930-1955. *GLQ: A Journal of Lesbian and Gay Studies, 4* [2], 159–187.

Moberly, E. R. (1986). Attachment and separation: the implications for gender identity and for the structuralization of the self: a theoretical model for transsexualism, and homosexuality. *Psychiatric Journal of the University of Ottawa, 11*(4), 205–209.

Modestin, J., & Ebner, G. (1995). Multiple personality disorder manifesting itself under the mask of transsexualism. *Psychopathology, 28*(6), 317–321.

Money, J. (1980). *Love and love sickness: The science of sex, gender differences, and pair-bonding.* Baltimore, MD: Johns Hopkins University Press.

Money, J. (1986). *Lovemaps: Clinical concepts of sexual/erotic health and pathology, paraphilia, and gender transposition in childhood, adolescence, and maturity.* New York: Irvington.

Money, J. (1994a). The concept of gender identity disorder in childhood and adolescence after 39 years. *Journal of Sex and Marital Therapy, 20*(3), 163–177.

Money, J. (1994b). *Sex errors of the body and related syndromes: A guide to counseling children, adolescents, and their families.* Baltimore: Paul H. Brookes.

Money, J., & Tucker, P. (1975). *Sexual signatures: On being a man or a woman.* Boston: Little, Brown.

Morris, J. (1974). *Conundrum.* New York: Harcourt Brace Jovanovich.

Murray, J. F. (1985). Borderline manifestations in the Rorschachs of male transsexuals. *Journal of Personality Assessment, 49*(5), 454–466.

Nathanson, D. (1992). *Shame and pride.* New York: Norton.

Ndirangu, K. (1993). Transsexual surgery: A case of true gender dysphoria. *East African Medical Journal, 70*(11), 737–738.

Nusselt, L., & Kockott, G. (1976). [Electroencephalographic changes in transsexualism], (abstract), *EEG-EMG, 7*(1), 42–48.

References

Ousterhout, D. K. (1993). *Skull modification in the gender dysphoric patient*. Paper presented at the 13th international symposium on gender dysphoria, Harry Benjamin International Gender Dysphoria Association, New York.

Ovesey, L., & Person, E. (1976). Transvestism: A disorder of the sense of self. International *Journal of Psychoanalytic Psychotherapy, 5,* 219–236.

Pauly, I. B. (1965). Male psychosexual inversion: transsexualism. *Archives of General Psychiatry, 13,* 172–181.

Pauly, I. B. (1968). The current status of the change of sex operation. *Journal of Nervous and Mental Disorders, 147,* 460–471.

Pauly, I. B. (1981). Outcome of sex reassignment surgery for transsexuals. *Australian and New Zealand Journal of Psychiatry, 15,* 45–51.

Pauly, I. B. (1990). Gender identity disorders: evaluation and treatment. *Journal of Sex Education and Therapy, 16,* 2–24.

Pauly, I. B. (1992). Terminology and classification of gender identity disorders. In W. O. Bockting & E. Coleman (Eds.), *Gender dysphoria: interdisciplinary approaches in clinical management* (pp. 1–11). New York: Haworth.

Pauly, I. B., & Edgerton, M. T. (1986). The gender identity movement: a growing surgical-psychiatric liaison. *Archives of Sexual Behavior, 15*(4), 315–329.

Peo, R. E. (1988). Transvestism. *Journal of Social Work and Human Sexuality, 7,* 57–75.

Pfafflin, F. (1992). Regrets after sex reassignment surgery. In W. O. Bockting and E. Coleman (Eds.), *Gender dysphoria: Interdisciplinary approaches In clinical management* (pp. 69–85). New York: Hayworth.

Puri, B. K. & Singh, I. (1996). The successful treatment of a gender dysphoric patient with pimozide. *Australian and New Zealand Journal of Psychiatry, 30*(3), 422–425.

Rakic, Z., Starcevic, V., Maric, J., & Kelin, K. (1996). The outcome of sex reassignment surgery in Belgrade: 32 patients of both sexes. *Archives of Sexual Behavior, 25*(5), 515–525.

Rebec, G. (1998). From dopamine to vitamin C: What's novel? *Indiana University Department of Psychology Alumni Newsletter, 4.*

Robertson, C. E. (1989). The mahu of Hawaii. *Feminist Studies, 15,* 313–327.

Rogers, C. (1961). *On becoming a person.* Boston: Houghton Mifflin.

Ross, M. W., & Need, J. A. (1989). Effects of adequacy of gender reassignment surgery on psychological adjustment; a follow-up of fourteen male-to-female patients. *Archives of Sexual Behavior, 18*(2), 145–153.

Ross, M. W., Walinder, J., & Lundstrom, B. (1981). Cross-cultural approaches to transsexualism: a comparison between Sweden and Australia. *Acta Psychiatrica Scandinavica, 6* (1), 75–82.

Rothblatt, M. A. (1995). *The apartheid of sex: A manifesto on the freedom of gender.* New York: Crown.

Ruan, F. F., Bullough, V. L., & Tsai, Y. M. (1989). Male transsexualism in mainland China. *Archives of Sexual Behavior, 18*(6), 517–522.

Sadies, S. (Ed.), (1980). *The new Grove dictionary of music and musicians,* (Vol. 3, 875–876). London: Macmillan.

Schaefer, L. C., & Wheeler, C. C. (1983). *The non-surgery true transsexual, part II: Theoretical rationale.* Paper presented at the eighth international symposium on gender dysphoria, Harry Benjamin International Gender Dysphoria Association, Bordeaux: France.

Schaefer, L. C., & Wheeler, C. C. (1987a) *Tribute to Harry Benjamin, 1885–1986.* Paper presented at the tenth international symposium on gender dysphoria, Harry Benjamin International Gender Dysphoria Association. Amsterdam, The Netherlands.

Schaefer, L.C., & Wheeler, C.C. (1987b, June). *Harry Benjamin's early cases, 1938–1953: Historical influences, part 1.* Paper presented at the eighth World Congress for Sexology. Heidelberg, Germany.

Schaefer, L. C., & Wheeler, C. C. (1995). Clinical historical notes: Harry Benjamin's first ten cases (1938-1953). *Archives of Sexual Behavior, 24,* 73–93.

Schaefer, L.C., & Wheeler, C.C. (in press). Guilt and gender identity disorders and condition: Understanding, recognizing, diagnosing, and its treatments. *Journal of the International Society for the Study of Personal Relationships.*

Schaefer, L. C., Wheeler, C. C., & Futterweit, W. (1995). Gender identity disorders [transsexualism]. In G. O. Gabbard (Series Ed.), *Treatments of psychiatric disorders* (Vol. 2, 2nd ed., pp. 2015–2079). Washington, DC: American Psychiatric Press.

Sex-change surgery halted at Johns Hopkins. (1979, August 14). *The Chicago Sun-Times,* p. 38.

Shtasel, T. F. (1979). Behavioral treatment of transsexualism: A case report. *Journal of Sex and Marital Therapy, 5*(4), 362–367.

Siegel, F. K. (1989). *Intoxication: Life in pursuit of artificial paradise.* New York: Dutton.

Snaith, P. Tarsh, M. J., & Reid, R. (1993). Sex reassignment surgery; a study of 141 Dutch transsexuals. *British Journal of Psychiatry, 162,* 681–685.

Socarides, C. W. (1969). Dr. Socarides replies. [Letter to the editor]. *American Journal of Psychiatry, 126*(2), 156.

Socarides, C. W. (1970). A psychoanalytic study of the desire for sexual transformation [transsexualism]; the plaster-of-paris man. *The International Journal of Psycho-Analysis, 51*(3), 341–349.

Socarides, C. W. (1978). Transsexualism and psychosis. *International Journal of Psychoanalytic Psychotherapy, 7,* 373–384.

Solomon, R. L. (1980). The opponent-process theory of acquired motivation. *American Psychologist, 35,* 691–712.

References

Soutoul, J. H., Touze, M., & Froge, E. (1986). [The French physician and judge confronting the transsexual in 1986]. *Journal De Gynecologie, Obstetrique, Et Biologie De La Reproduction,15*(7), 873–875.

Spinder, T., Spijkstra, J. J., Gooren, L. J., & Burger, C. W. (1989). Pulsatile leuteinizing hormone release and ovarian steroid levels in female-to-male transsexuals compared to heterosexual women. *Psychneuroendocrinology, 14*(1-2), 97–102.

Spoljar, M., Eicher, W., Eiermann, W., & Cleve, H. (1981). H-Y antigen expression in different tissues from transsexuals. *Human Genetics, 57* (1), 52–57.

Stein, M., Tiefer, L., & Melman, A. (1990). Followup observations of operated male-to-female transsexuals. *Journal of Urology, 143*(6), 1188–1192.

Steiner, B. W., & Bernstein, S. M. (1981). Female-to-male transsexuals and their partners. *Canadian Journal of Psychiatry, 26*(3), 178–182.

Stevenson, I. (1977). The Southeast Asian interpretation of gender dysphoria: an illustrative case report. *Journal of Nervous and Mental Disease, 165*(3), 201–208.

Stoller, R. J. (1966). The mother's contribution to infantile transvestic behavior. *International Journal of Psychoanalysis, 47,* 384–395.

Stoller, R. J. (1969). Parental influences in male transsexualism. In R. Green & J. Money (Eds.), *Transsexualism and sex reassignment* (pp. 153–169). Baltimore: Johns Hopkins Univeristy Press.

Stoller, R. J. (1975). *Perversion, the erotic form of hatred.* New York: Pantheon.

Stoller, R. J. (1985). *Presentations of gender.* New Haven, CT: Yale University Press.

Sullivan, H. S. (1953). *The interpersonal theory of psychiatry.* New York: Norton.

Sullivan, L. (1990). *From female to male: The life of Jack Bee Garland.* Boston: Alyson Publications.

Sutton R. (1970). *The prairie state: The colonial years to 1860.* Grand Rapids, MI: Erdmous.

Taylor, T. (1996). *The prehistory of sex: Four million years of human sexual culture.* New York: Bantam.

Temple, R. (Ed.). (1998). *Aesop: The complete fables.* London: Bantam.

Tsoi, W. F. (1988). The prevalence of transsexualism in Singapore. *Acta Psychiatrica Scandinavica, 78*(4), 501–504.

Tsoi, W. F., Kok, L. P., Yeo, K. L., & Ratnam, S. S. (1995). Follow-up study of female transsexuals. *Annals of the Academy of Medicine, Singapore, 24*(5), 664–667.

Tsushima, W. T., & Wedding, D. (1979). MMPI results of male candidates for transsexual surgery. *Journal of Personality Assessment, 43*(4), 385–387.

Uddenberg, N., Walinder, J., & Hojerback, T. (1979). Parental contact in male and female transsexuals. *Acta psychiatrica Scandinavica, 60* (1),113–120.

van Kesteren, P. J., Gooren, L. J., & Megens, J. A. (1996). An epidemiological and demographic study of transsexuals in the Netherlands. *Archives of Sexual Behavior, 25*(6), 589–600.

van-Straalen, W. R., Hage, J. J., & Bloemena, E. (1995). The inframammary ligament: Myth or reality? *Annals of Plastic Surgery, 35*(3), 237–241.

Vatsyayana (1961). *Kama Sutra* (Upadhyaya, S. C., Trans.). Bombay: D. B. Taraporevala Sons.

Vogel, F. (1981). Neurobiological approaches in human behavior genetics. *Behavior Genetics, 11*(2), 87–102.

Wachtel, S., Green, R., Simon, N. G., Reichart, A., Cahill, L., Hall, J., Nakumura, D., Wachtel, G., Futterweit, W., & Biber, S. H. (1986). On the expression of the H-Y antigen in transsexuals. *Archives of Sexual Behavior, 15*(1), 51–68.

Walker, P., Berger, J., Green, R., et al. (1985). Standards of care; the hormonal and surgical sex reassignment of gender dysphoric persons. *Archives of Sexual Behavior, 14,* 79–90.

Watson, D. B., & Coren, S. (1992). Left-handedness in male-to-female transsexuals [letter]. *Journal of the American Medical Association,* 267(10), 1342.

Weitze, C., & Osburg, S. (1996). Transsexualism in Germany: Empirical data on epidemiology and application of the German Transsexuals' Act during its first ten years. *Archives of Sexual Behavior,* 25(4), 409–425.

White, T. G., (1997). *Gender identity disorder: Nature, nurture and a common final pathway.* Paper presented at the Second International Congress on Sex and Gender, King of Prussia, Pennsylvania.

Williams, W. L. (1986). *The spirit and the flesh: Sexual diversity in American Indian culture.* Boston: Beacon Press.

Wu, C. (1995, August 26). Ancient crocodile chomped on plants. *Science News,* p. 132.

Yuksel, S., Sahin, D., Karali, N., & Baral, I. (1995). *Doing group psychotherapy with female-to-male transsexuals in Turkey.* Paper presented at the fourteenth international symposium on gender dysphoria, Harry Benjamin International Gender Dysphoria Association, Germany.

Zhou, J. N., Hofman, M. A., Gooren, L. J., & Swaab, D. F. (1995). A sex difference in the human brain and its relation to transsexuality. *Nature, 378*(6552), 68–70.

Zucker, K. J., & Bradley, S. J. (1995). *Gender identity disorder and psychosexual problems in children and adolescents.* New York: Guilford.

Zucker, K. J., Bradley, S. J., Oliver, G., Blake, J., Fleming, S., & Hood, J. (1996). Psychosexual development of women with congenital adrenal hyperplasia. *Hormones and Behavior, 30*(4), 300–318.

Index

Index